CLASSIC GIN

GERALDINE COATES

First published in 2000 in Great Britain by
Prion Books Limited, Imperial Works, Perren Street
London NW5 3ED

© 2000 Prion Books Ltd
Text copyright © Geraldine Coates

ISBN 1-85375-334-3

Cover design: Bob Eames

Printed and bound in China

ACKNOWLEDGEMENTS

I would like to thank all those who helped with the writing of this
book. They include:

Ananda Brown; Robert Grieve; Alex Field; Hugh Williams of
United Distillers; Desmond Payne of Beefeater; The Gin and
Vodka Association of Great Britain; The Plymouth Distillery;
Henk Iprenburg and Drs. Jack Verheok at PGD, Schiedam; M.
Jansen at De Kuyper, Schiedam; Staff at The Museum Distillery,
Schiedam; Piet van Leijenhorst and Tom Vermeulen at Bols Royal
Distillerie; Zeb, Beth and Morgan Coates; Simon Difford at *Class*;
Christopher and Sarah Boisseau; Charles Maclean; Martin Gill;
Diane Arrowsmith of G & J Greenalls; Jane Ewing and Deborah
Charnock at United Distillers; The UDV Archive in Leven, Fife;
Mirjam Huggins; Edward Jones; Prue Irvine, author of *Easy Peasy*,
and The Cook's Bookshop.

CLASSIC GIN

In the same series:

CONTENTS

INTRODUCTION

Gin is one of the world's great spirits and yet it is a spirit which is inherently schizophrenic. It is the basis for what has been described as America's contribution to civilisation – the silver bullet, otherwise known as the dry martini. At the same time, even the very word can conjure up images of loucheness and despair – hence 'mother's ruin', 'cuckold's comfort' and other names whose negative associations gin has never quite shaken off. To some gin is the tart with a heart: to others a glamourous ice queen.

One reason for this dual nature is that gin has led an interesting life. Its prototype was a juniper based cordial in 14th century Flanders, reputed to protect against the Black Death. People not only drank the wonder potion, they wore masks filled with juniper berries so that even the air they breathed would be purified by the magical herb. The Dutch and Flemish called their new drink "jenever" and it came to England as "gin" when Dutch William of Orange accepted the English Crown in 1689. Gin soon became immensely popular. By the early 18th-century the Gin craze was at its height and it was the principle solace of the poor in the slums of English cities much to the dismay of contemporary social reformers.

Opposite
A 1930s
American ad
evokes the
nostalgic quality
of gin – a drink
for all times.

Gin rose from these lowly origins to become the ultimate in sophistication. This book traces each step of the astonishing rise; from the legislative chaos that governed the first attempts to reform gin distilling, to the development of the London Dry style and the ascent of the great 19th-century distilling houses, through Prohibition and the first Cocktail Age, to the revival of cocktail culture in the 1990s.

It's not only its history that makes gin interesting. Gin is a drinker's drink in a world where increasingly, neutral, bland tastes are becoming the norm. Whether as the base of a classic cocktail or in a long drink, gin makes its presence felt in no uncertain terms. That's one reason why it is currently enjoying such a revival in its fortunes, a revival which is led by premium style, high strength gins. Gin has shaken off its old fogey image and become once again a drink for drinkers who seek flavour, character and heritage.

Certainly gin is part of the English heritage. The English perfected gin as we know it today and it is still perceived as English in a way no other spirit is. Moreover, gin encapsulates the English tradition of internationalism. Consider first the exotic ingredients of the botanical mixes, which come from the far corners of the world – corners where the English have traded for over four hundred years. Consider, too, the prestige that English gin has enjoyed in export markets ever since Felix Booth had the fore sight to persuade Parliament to lift taxes on export gin in 1850. And when, in the 1960s and 70s it seemed that gin was losing its position as the predominant white spirit, it was to English distillers that the international marketing gurus turned to create new stylish gins to compete with vodka.

Gin is also truly global – known and appreciated all round the world, as any barman anywhere will tell you. It has had its famous admirers, particularly among the reckless: Byron, Rimbaud, F Scott Fitzgerald, Faulkner, Hemingway, the "Bright Young Things", the literati of the Algonquin Round Table, the Hollywood Rat Pack, the Rolling Stones – each has a story to tell about gin.

Drinking gin is one of life's great pleasures which, like other pleasures, is enhanced by knowing more. This book is intended to reveal more about gin: its history and culture; how it's made, the premium established brands, the best of the newcomers to the market and gin oddities; and how to enjoy gin in mixed drinks and food.

Geraldine Coates
2000

EARLY HISTORY

THE FIRST DISTILLERS

Gin is made by a process no different in principle from the distilling techniques used thousands of years ago. Eight centuries before Christ, the Chinese were making *sautchoo* from fermented rice alcohol, the Tartars were producing *arika* from fermented mare's milk, and the Sinhalese were distilling *arrack* from coconut toddy. However, written records of early distilling are almost non-existent. Aristotle writes in AD4 of the practice of distilling sea water to produce drinking water. Then a long silence until early in the 9th century when Rhazes, an Arab philosopher, recognised the potential of distilled alcohol as a medium for medicinal herbs and berries.

Most authorities hold that the Arabs brought the secrets of distilling to mainland Europe some time during the Moorish occupation of Spain. The knowledge then seems to have gradually spread from southern Europe northwards.

While the Arabs were intrigued by the metaphysical and medical significance of distilling and associated the spirit produced with the Divine, another strand of distilling activity in the Celtic badlands of Europe was more concerned with earthly matters. St. Patrick is believed to have introduced the still to Ireland during his mission of AD432. Irish monks exported distilling skills to the west of Scotland some time in the 6th century and there is evidence that, in both Ireland and Scotland, production and consumption of spirits were part of daily life. Certainly the Normans found distillation from grain firmly established when they invaded in the 12th century.

THE MONASTIC TRADITION

How desirable and convenient it would be if, from the time of the introduction of distilled alcohol into Europe, one could find dates, places and written evidence that would allow us to trace the development of each country's national drink. Sadly we cannot: there are no names, there is no pack drill.

Above

An early label from the Plymouth Gin brand sports its trademark 'blackfriar' after which its distillery was named.

11

Occasionally the mists part. We know that by the early 11th century the Benedictine monks of Salerno in Italy had rediscovered the writings of Greek and Arab scholars and were distilling spirits along with various herbs, spices, berries and roots to create medicines and remedies. The Salerno monks codified the uses of these natural remedies and experimented freely with whatever was to hand. Although no recipe survives, we can safely assume that, because juniper grows so rampantly all over Italy, they would have developed a juniper-based spirit to use as a potion, particularly as juniper's diuretic effects were already known and it was widely used in the treatment of kidney and bladder diseases. So the most likely candidate as the first producer of a proto-gin appears to be an anonymous monk in the kitchens of a Benedictine monastery in about AD1050.

During the Dark Ages, like much other arcane knowledge, distilling seems to have disappeared from mainland Europe. It was rediscovered by Arnold de Villa Nova, a 13th-century alchemist who taught at the universities of Montpelier and Avignon. He is credited as being the father of distilling and wrote in his *Boke of Wine* of the distillation of wine into 'aqua vitae' and its subsequent flavouring with various herbs and spices. His description – 'the water of life' – has entered every European language: *eau de vie* in French, *agua ardente* in Italian, *akvavit* in Swedish, *usquebaugh* in Gaelic (from whence comes 'whisky').

This rebirth of European distilling took place in the kitchens of mediaeval monasteries and was almost exclusively concentrated on the manufacture of medicinal cordials and liqueurs. Aqua vitae itself was considered to be of great therapeutic value and it was noticed that the rich,

who tended to drink more freely of wine and spirits, had better health and lived longer. (What no one realised then is that they probably drank less water, which was the chief carrier of disease.) The spirit itself was taken as a medicine, and combined with other flavourings and then redistilled to make marvellous elixirs and potions. Small-scale industries grew up, some of whose

Above
The rebirth of European distilling took place in the kitchens of mediaeval monasteries.

Below

Juniper berries had long been used for medicinal purposes before their appearance in the first 'gins'.

products still survive – Benedictine for example, and Chartreuse, originally an 'elixir of long life', which has been produced continuously at the same location since 1605.

THE USE OF JUNIPER

Cordials and elixirs based on juniper began to be widely used during the 14th century. It acquired the status of a wonder drug that could protect against the deadly bubonic plague, hence its prophylactic use during the years of the Black Death when epidemics of plague stalked Europe, killing over 25 million people. Distilling by this time had broken out of its monastic confines into the still-rooms of the great European noble houses, where domestic duties included the production of aromatic cordials and liqueurs. A contemporary recipe from *Delights for Ladies*, a mediaeval recipe book, gives instructions for a preparation containing juniper: 'Distill with a gentle heat either in balneo, or ashes, the strong and sweet water wherewith you have drawen oil of cloves, mace, nutmegs, iuniper, rosemarie, &c. after it hath stood one moneth close stopt, and so you shall purchase a delicate spirit of each of the said aromaticall bodies.' Scientifically minded aristocrats, drawn to distilling because of its alchemical, almost magical, connotations, experimented endlessly. Another proto-gin appeared when a son of Henri IV of France distilled wine with juniper. It was drunk in France in the 15th century and was known as 'the wine of the poor'.

Tantalising though these glimpses into gin's origins are, we are still far removed from a true gin – a grain spirit flavoured with juniper. These juniper-flavoured drinks were based on a distillation of wine: in the cold and dank, vineless climates of Northern Europe it was a different story.

DISTILLING IN NORTHERN EUROPE

By the 14th century it was generally realised that potable spirits could be made from locally available crops such as fruits, potatoes, rye and barley. At the same time distilling was no longer the sole domain of the dabbler, the scholar, the scientist or the medicine man. Ordinary people discovered it, firstly as a way to make use of an abundant harvest in times of plenty, and secondly as a foolproof method of mitigating the harshness of lives that were all too often nasty, brutish and short. From then on, therefore, it begins to be possible to chronicle the evolution of European spirits from cottage industries to proud national symbols – vodka in Russia and

Poland, whisky in Scotland and Ireland, brandy in France, schnapps in Germany, and gin first in the Low Countries and later in England.

JENEVER IN THE LOW COUNTRIES

If you read anything about the early history of gin, almost all the sources will tell you that Sylvius of Leyden, Professor of Medicine at the University of Leyden in 1572, was the first to perfect a juniper-flavoured grain spirit. This is complete nonsense, a marketing wheeze dreamed up in the 1960s by an over-imaginative copy-

writer. Juniper-flavoured distillates, as we have seen, had made several appearances long before Sylvius' time and, by the 15th century, the practice of flavouring spirit with juniper had entered the Low Countries (Holland, Belgium and parts of Northern France that became separate countries only in the 1880s) via Flanders.

There survive records in the Low Countries from the 15th century onwards of the regulations issued and the taxes imposed on the numerous small distilleries making spirits from wine and from grain. Excise records of 1492 in Amsterdam, for example, confirm the production of significant quantities of spirit from cereals,

Above

Amsterdam was the major port through which sugar and spices entered Northern Europe from the East and West Indies. It soon became a centre for distilling, chiefly liqueurs, and in a smaller way, jenever.

mainly rye, known as *brandewijn* (Dutch for burnt or heated wine), the term for all forms of spirit. Constant experimentation was carried out to find a way of masking the fusel oil flavours of brandewijn to make it more palatable. Juniper combined well with it, particularly when it was sweetened with sugar, had the advantage of

growing everywhere in the Low Countries, and was considered to be restorative and life-giving. And so *jenever*, from the French *genievre* ('juniper'), came into being. It was a marriage of the Celtic tradition of making alcohol from crops in the field to drink for pleasure and the monastic tradition of experimenting with different ingredients to create medicines.

One reason why jenever was soon established as the Dutch/Belgian national drink was that a large-scale national distilling industry and a huge export trade in spirits were soon developed. In the years between 1500 and 1700 distilleries were established in every town and distilling became as distinctively Dutch as cheese-making and tobacco. Foreigners claimed that it was the foul climate of the Low Countries that made drinking so much a part of life but there were other reasons. The innate Dutch inventiveness and love of experimentation meant that there was virtually no ingredient they would not distil into strong drink. Crucially, there was a surplus of wine, grain and the other ingre-dients distillers needed. The Dutch had a vast maritime empire based on

Opposite
In the 16th century the jenever industry moved lock, stock and barrel out of Rotterdam, the principle grain port of the Low Countries, to its satellite town, Schiedam. In its heyday Schiedam could boast over 400 distilleries.

trade and, every hour of every day, the ships of the East and West Indies companies unloaded precious cargoes of goods and foodstuffs from all over the world into the ports of the Low Countries. In return, the Dutch carried spirits, cognac, a spirit whose commercial production the Dutch had initiated, and jenever, their home grown spirit, to the ports of Northern Europe, Indonesia, the Caribbean, West Africa – anywhere there was a deal to be done. In the 16th century Amsterdam became the pre-eminent port for sugar and spices and a centre for liqueur making. Rotterdam was the grain port and Schiedam, its satellite town, became the hub of jenever production.

JENEVER COMES TO ENGLAND

During the Thirty Years War (1618–48), the Low Countries were the battlefields of Europe as the armies of France, England and Spain fought over bitterly disputed territory. The long drawn-out campaigns in miserable conditions lasted many months and the English soldiers became familiar with the strong, distinctive-tasting local grog, often taken as a morale-boosting slug before battle. They appreciated this Dutch courage and when the wars in Europe finally came to an end they brought home the taste for jenever, or gin, as they had begun to call it.

In England spirits had been distilled in a small way since Tudor times. Whisky production and drinking was confined to Scotland and Ireland and, because the English had always relied on cheap imports of French brandy, they had never developed large-scale domestic distilling concerns of their own. However, there are frequent early 17th-century references to 'aqua vitae', a crude distilled spirit made from fermented grain, fruit, wine dregs or old cider, and by 1621 there were 200 establishments in the cities of London and Westminster distilling aqua vitae and 'other strong and hott waters', mainly for medicinal purposes.

The father of English distilling was Sir Theodore De Mayerne, a noted physician and alchemist. In 1638, under the reign of Charles I, Sir Theodore and Thomas Cademan, physician to the Queen, founded The Company of Distillers. They obtained for the Company a Royal Charter, which conferred exclusive powers to distil spirits and vinegar in London and Westminster and within a radius of 21 miles, and they codified the rules and standards of distillation in their publication *The Distiller of London*. Most of the Company's distilling principles were negated by subsequent legislation but their insistence on the rectification of spirits and ban on the sale of 'low spirits' laid the groundwork for a later return to quality.

Throughout the latter half of the 17th century gin was distilled in small quantities, chiefly as a medicine. In Pepys's famous diary, the entry for 10 October 1663 reads: 'Sir W. Batten did advise me to take some juniper water…strong water made of juniper.' The fact that Pepys, well known as a man of fashion and bon viveur, never referred to gin being drunk for pleasure is a fairly reliable sign that it was not socially drunk. No doubt soldiers and sailors in the English ports and the six thousand Dutchmen living in London at the time could have enlightened him. Gin continued to remain a secret, known to only a few.

THE REVOLUTION

What changed this was the arrival of a Dutchman to the English throne in 1688, the year of the Glorious Revolution. The most immediate result of the replacement of the unpopular Stewart king James II with Dutch Protestant William of Orange, who was married to James's daughter Mary, was that

everything Catholic and French was out and all things Protestant and Dutch were in.

A powerful cabal of land-owners, many of whom had helped William to the throne, and anti-French, anti-Catholic interests pushed the 1690 Distilling Act through Parliament. It was to have an enormous impact on drinking habits for centuries by introducing legislation to ban French imports of wine and brandy and encouraging the distillation of 'good and whole-some brandies, aqua vitae and spirits, drawn and made from malted corn'.

The Act created the economic conditions for an English distilling industry. Farmers and land-owners were delighted because the new Act allowed them to sell surplus crops at a profit. It also partially negated the monopoly that had earlier been granted to the Worshipful Company of Distillers. From now on distilling was open to all, once a public notice of the intention to distil had been posted for at least ten days.

Other strategic pieces of legislation were a further boost to the development of the distilling industry. The raising of taxes on beer in 1694 made spirits cheaper than beer for the first time and, in 1702, the withdrawal of the remaining monopoly of the Distillers Company opened up home-grown distilling even further. The 1720 Mutiny Act excused tradesmen who were distil-lers from having soldiers billeted on them, even more of an encouragement to enter the field.

There was clearly now every reason for distilling in early 18th-century England to flourish but why that new industry should have flung itself so wholeheartedly into the production of gin is not so obvious. Perhaps England's headlong rush into the mad years of the Gin Craze was, like many other crazes, fuelled simply by fashion and greed.

The fashion for gin drinking was led by King Billy and his mainly Dutch Court. In the new, more egalitarian, more democratic England that had emerged from the bloodless revolution, gin drinking was considered a sign of patriotism and Protestantism. It became a symbol of a desire to set aside the old religious and political arguments that had dominated the century, itself now drawing to a close, and to embrace all things modern. Like the king, gin was new, Dutch and progressive, and the English took to both like ducks to water. Gin became the people's drink.

The conditions were already established in which virtually anyone who wished to could climb on board the distilling bandwagon and profit from the new fashion for drinking spirits. What then could be more of a gift to greedy, unscrupulous distillers than a heavily sweetened, dual-natured drink in which the strong flavour of juniper and other spices could hide a multitude of sins? The stage was set.

GIN LANE.

THE GIN CRAZE

It is almost impossible to overemphasise the extent to which gin drinking in England in the early 18th century became an epidemic. Compare it with the scourge of crack cocaine in American inner cities in the 1980s and one begins to get the picture. In 1689 the whole of England produced at most only half a million gallons of gin a year. In 1727 the consumption of gin reached 5 million gallons: by 1733 official figures confirmed that that year London alone produced 11 million gallons of gin – 14 gallons for every resident – not including home-made gin produced from the hundreds of illegal stills. By 1730 in London there were over 7,000 dram shops; in some parts of the city one house in three sold gin. With no means of controlling either those who produced gin or those who sold it, gin was universally available – and universally consumed.

It's easy to see the attraction. Living and working conditions for those at the bottom of the 18th-century social heap were appalling. Gin provided a temporary escape – at a price. Hogarth's 'Gin Lane' sums it up – in the foreground the child falling unnoticed from the arms of its drunken mother, the pawn shop besieged by desperate customers, the crowd storming the gin shop, the wraith-like figure of Death dominating images of chaos and despair. This powerful piece of propaganda supported

Opposite

Hogarth's Gin Lane *captures all that was tragic and corrupt in the wake of the unprecedented 'Gin Craze'.*

shocking contemporary statistics. For example, in 1723 the death rate in London outstripped the birth rate and remained higher for the next ten years; in the years between 1730 and 1749, 75 per cent of all the children christened in London were buried before the age of five; and in London between 1740 and 1742 there were two burials to every baptism. The children of the poor were dying like flies.

Records speak of the hospices and hospitals in the City packed with 'increasing multitudes of dropsical and consumptive people arising from the effects of spirituous liquors' and certainly gin itself was blamed for lowering fertility and causing birth defects and neglectful parenting (this perhaps explains how the term 'mother's ruin' came about). Contemporary commentators were appalled. Tobias Smollett, in his *History of England*, gave a much-quoted description of gin drinking: 'The retailers of this poisonous compound set up painted boards in public inviting people to be drunk for the small expense of one penny, assuring them they might be dead drunk for two pence and have straw for nothing. They accordingly provided cellars and places strewed with straw to which they conveyed those wretches who were overwhelmed with intoxication.' Not an attractive picture. Something had to be done.

In response to the public concerns raised, well-meant but ill-considered attempts were made to control the gin madness. Most surprising of all was

Right
*An inn sign
shows the
allegorical
figure of gin,
Madame
Geneva, as a
burden to the
drinking man.*

the decree that only dwelling houses could sell 'intoxicating liquors'. It had predictable consequences – even more homes became gin shops. The Act of 1736 – which attempted to fix a licence fee of £50 for gin retailers, prohibited the sale of gin in quantities under 2 gallons and taxed it at £1 per gallon – caused the most outrage. There were riots and unrest all over the country and mock funeral processions carrying effigies of Madam Geneva took place the night before the Act became law.

Above *A London Gin Palace in 1820 by George Cruikshank.*
Note the barrels marked 'Old Tom'.

In truth the 1736 Act demonstrated, as Prohibition was to do nearly two hundred years later, how foolish the law can be when it is unenforceable. Only two of the £50 licences were ever taken out. Wine licences had remained at only a few shillings so many gin shops transformed themselves overnight into 'wine merchants', selling gin with a splash of wine under names such as Sangaree, Tow Row, Ladies' Delight, Cuckolds Comfort, and a 'new' drink satirically christened 'Parliamentary Brandy'. Sales of illicit gin were higher than ever and Parliament was forced to repeal the Act in 1742.

EFFECTIVE LEGISLATION AND CONTROL

In 1743 the Government introduced yet another Gin Act. This one achieved the right balance between a genuine desire for control over gin – badly needed, given that London was now producing 20 million gallons of gin annually for a population of 500,000 – and pragmatism. Licences of £1 to sell gin were to be granted to holders of beer and ale licences and distillers were not allowed to retail gin direct to the public but only to licensed houses. Rather than trying to enforce a form of prohibition, Parliament was pursuing the far more realistic goals of moderation and proper controls.

Spurred on by the success of this Act and a rising anti-gin crusade, in 1751 Parliament passed a law known as the Tippling Act: only established licensed public houses could sell gin; if credit was given to customers, sums under £1 were not recoverable in law; and chandlers and those in charge of gaols and poor-houses were specifically forbidden to retail alcohol.

By further controlling those who could sell gin and by raising excise duties to a level that would discourage the back-street boys, the Tippling Act dragged gin out of the gutter. Taxes and duties on gin began to produce a valuable source of revenue for the public purse and the excise duty on spirits was raised steadily – from £7 7s 0d in 1751 to £61 19s 9d in 1791. Prices rose correspondingly, and consumption fell. During the years of bad harvest between 1757 and 1760, the distillation of spirits from corn was prohibited. Prices shot up dramatically, with such beneficial effects on the well-being of the common people that Parliament was inundated with demands that the prohibition should be permanent. The farmers protested vociferously, a compromise was reached, and the duty was raised yet again.

Ever-increasing excise duties meant gin was no longer cheap, no longer the opium of the masses. Proper controls and regulations led to the proper supervision and management of distilling. This encouraged respectable companies to begin making quality products and it is no coincidence that the rise of the great English distilling houses dates from this time.

GIN IN THE 19TH CENTURY

Opposite
An early gin palace as seen through the eyes of George Cruikshank, Dickens' illustrator and a famous temperancer. Notice the small child handing up a bottle to be filled.

Lord Kinross, in his book *The Kindred Spirit* (pub 1959), gives a marvellous description of gin as the 'ardent spirit which rose from the gutter to become the respectable companion of civilised man'. That rise was accomplished through the combination of a fundamental evolution in the drink itself with a broader change in social conditions and attitudes towards drinking. It started in the 19th century.

OLD TOM

The gin that fuelled the gin craze resembled a cordial, heavily sweetened with sugar and glycerine and strongly flavoured with juniper and other herbs to conceal off flavours in the spirit. The most popular brand and the one that eventually defined this style was Old Tom, a name for which there are several explanations. Its most attractive provenance concerned Captain Dudley Bradstreet, an enterprising informer turned bootlegger who took advantage of a loophole in the 1736 Act that stipulated that an

CHAPTER TWO

Opposite

Gordon's was one of the first distilling firms to flourish under the new controls and regulations of the 19th century.

informer must know the name of the owner of rented property from which illegal gin was sold. He acquired a property whose ownership was in dispute and invested £13 in a stock of gin from Langdale's distillery in Holborn. Under a trade sign depicting a cat (an 'old tom'), he installed a slot and a lead pipe, one end of which was located under the cat's paw. To the other end, inside the house, he attached a funnel. Customers placed their money in the slot and duly received their gin. His business prospered until competition became too stiff. As he recorded: 'My Scheme of Puss, now becoming common, was practised by many others, which greatly diminished my Business and made me drop it, and turn my Head to something else.'

All the distilling companies produced an Old Tom style gin until fairly recently. One was made by Gordon's until the 1970s and, according to Dave Broome, author of the masterly *Spirits & Cocktails*, Old Tom style gin can still be found in Finland. The best way of getting an idea of what this type of gin tasted like is to try a Dutch oude jenever (see page 126).

THE RISE OF THE GREAT HOUSES

The gradual displacement of heavy, sweet gin by the unsweetened, clear, less aromatic gin in what came to be known as the London Dry style can be attributed to various factors. Perhaps the most significant was the invention in 1832 of the continuous still (see page 64), which allowed a purer, more consistent spirit to be made. The flavour of the spirit did not now need to be disguised but could instead be enhanced with the right combination of flavourings.

Control and regulation of distilling had encouraged responsible firms to become involved and, by the 19th century, there were about six large distilling firms and several smaller ones, based in London and producing quality products. Of them Booth's and Boord's were the largest producers and Gordon's was already prominent.

London's early domination of the distilling industry was due to the purity of the water to be found in its (then) outlying villages, like Clerkenwell (Clerk's Well) and Bloomsbury. Booth's had been established in Clerkenwell probably as early as 1740 and Sir Robert Burnett (Burnett's White Satin) in 1770. Gordon's was founded in Southwark in 1769, moving to Clerkenwell in 1798. By 1830 Charles Tanqueray had established his distillery in Bloomsbury. James Burrough began production of Beefeater gin in Chelsea in 1863,

and the Gilbeys were in business by 1872. These firms, which remain the names of our leading brands today and others formed the nucleus of what could now properly be described as a distilling industry.

London, with its ever-changing social patterns and constant influx of new money, afforded opportunities for these merchant families to rise socially. As the waspish Boswell commented in his *Life of Samuel Johnson*, 'Foreigners are not a little amazed when they hear of brewers, distillers and men in similar departments of trade held forth as persons of considerable consequence.' But it was so, and, because their reputations rested on the quality of their products, these gentlemen distillers became obsessed with quality.

From about the mid-19th century we find firms like Gordon's sourcing their base spirit from grain whisky producers in Scotland and an increasing emphasis on quality methods of production and quality ingredients. The Haigs and Steins, who dominated the legal distilling industry in Scotland, first dabbled in the gin trade in 1777, exporting 2,000 gallons of grain spirit to London. By 1782 this had risen to 184,000 gallons. Legislation of 1823 transformed Scottish distilling by halving duties and permitting volume production of a better quality of spirit. Licensed production of malt and grain spirit increased greatly and much of this soon found its way south of the Border for

Opposite
Hogarth's Beer Street, *where order, quiet and peace preside, is the antithesis of his apocalyptic* Gin Lane.

rectification into gin, despite screams of protest from English distillers and maltsters.

DRINKING HABITS IN THE 19TH CENTURY

Throughout the 18th century one thing those at the top of the social scale and those at the bottom had in common was a love of excessive drinking. In 1773 Dr Johnson spoke of a time when 'all the decent people in Lichfield got drunk every night and were not thought the worse off'. Once cheap gin disappeared, drinking habits became more moderate, but gin remained a feature of working-class life.

One should not forget that the companion piece to Hogarth's 'Gin Lane' was 'Beer Street', where all was quiet, orderly and peaceful. As part of the anti-gin drive the brewing and consumption of beer had been actively encouraged and by 1836 there was a total of 56,000 licensed beer shops in England and Wales. Many of these were ramshackle shebeens, and magistrates demanded improvements before granting and renewing licences. Landlords often borrowed money from the brewers for the improvements, promising in return to buy supplies exclusively from them. And so began the 'tied house' system that was indirectly to have a major effect on gin's rise to respectability.

PALACES OF THE PEOPLE

By 1816 half the victualling houses in London were tied, and brewers were building new, more up-market premises intended to draw in the passing trade. Desperate to compete, the gin shops upped the ante, transforming themselves into oases of glamour – people's palaces where ordinary folk could escape their wretched surroundings. The more sordid and squalid the neighbourhood, the more numerous and luxurious were its gin palaces. Dickens's contemporary description of a gin palace, in a squalid street in Holborn or Cheapside, deserves quoting in full:

'You turn the corner. What a change. All is light and brilliancy. The hum of many voices issues from that splendid gin-shop which forms the commencement of the two streets opposite; and the gay building with the fantastically ornamented parapet, the illuminated clock, the plate-glass windows surrounded by stucco rosettes, and its profusion of gas-lights in richly-gilt burners, is perfectly dazzling when contrasted with the dirt and dark we have just left. The interior is even gayer than the exterior. A bar of French-polished mahogany, elegantly-carved, extends the whole width of the place; and there are two side-aisles of great casks, painted green and gold, and bearing such inscriptions as 'Old Tom, 549'; 'Young Tom, 360'; 'Samson, 1421' the figures agreeing, we presume, with 'gallons', understand. Beyond the bar is a lofty and spacious saloon, full of the same enticing vessels, with a gallery running round it, equally well furnished. On the counter, in addition to the usual spirit apparatus, are two or three little baskets of cakes and biscuits which are carefully secured at the top with wicker-work to prevent their contents being unlawfully extracted.'

from *Sketches by Boz*

Above

A vision of mahogany and etched glass, the façade of The Prince Alfred in west London is a well-preserved example of the Victorian gin palace.

Gin palaces were urban. The first to open in London was probably that of Fearon's in Holborn Hill in about 1830. Soon they were a feature of life in industrial cities. In fact many fine examples remain: The Barley Mow and The Warrington Hotel in London; The Cafe Royal in Edinburgh; The Horseshoe in Glasgow; and, perhaps one of the most famous bars in the world, The Crown in Belfast, now owned by the National Trust who spent over £400,000 to restore it to its original palatial glory.

The attraction of gin palaces was that they provided what home often lacked – brightness, warmth, comfort, and easy companionship. Some of their glamour rubbed off on gin itself and contributed to a change in drinking culture to view drinking as a social pleasure not merely a shortcut to oblivion. But not everyone agreed: one has only to look at the drawings of George Cruikshank, Dickens's illustrator, for the moralists' point of view.

THE TEMPERANCE LOBBY

Cruikshank was not alone. A major change in attitudes to drink and drinking came about in Victorian England because of the development of a well-organised anti-drink lobby. Ironically enough, however, the final result was the exact opposite of what the temperancers had intended.

The British Temperance movement started in Preston, Lancashire in 1832 with the signing of the first total abstinence pledge. Despite the thousands who signed the pledge at mass rallies and the influential movers who joined the cause, temperancers and prohibitionists never achieved much real political power. They did, however,

Above
A propaganda envelope produced by the Temperance movement featuring satirical scenes from Hogarth and Cruikshank's line drawings.

succeed in securing pieces of legislation to control when, how, and by whom alcohol could be sold, much of which was beneficial. Who, for example, could argue with outlawing the practice of selling small children 'squibs' – the child-size portions of gin sold to 10-year-olds by unscrupulous landlords?

The failure of the temperancers to achieve their ultimate goal – a ban on the sale and consumption of alcohol – enshrined in British Law the right to drink, best summed up by the bishop who roundly declared, during yet another stormy licensing debate in the House of Lords, 'I would rather see England free than England sober'. When the Liberal government went to the country in 1874, it was decisively rejected by voters, bitter about Gladstone's capitulations to prohibitionism. 'We have been borne down in a torrent of gin,' the defeated Gladstone wrote. How unlike our American cousins, who were shortly to embark on their 'noble experiment'.

INCREASING RESPECTABILITY

Once the principle of moderate drinking was established in law and the stigma attached to gin drinking in particular began to disappear, the new, essentially middle-class style of gin quickly found middle-class devotees, particularly among women. In 1861 licences to sell alcohol were granted to retailers. By 1872 the temperance societies were up in arms about 'grocers' gin', citing cases like that of the Ipswich shop that sold 100 bottles of gin a week almost exclusively to women. Many of these were genteel Victorian ladies who served gin at tea parties from decanters labelled 'nig', and coyly calling it 'white wine'.

Gin's respectability was further increased when it became an important export. Until the mid-19th century, all UK-produced gin was for the domestic market. Heavy excise duties had handicapped the export trade until, in 1850, Sir Felix Booth of the Booth distilling family spent a small fortune on pushing a Private Bill through Parliament to remove excise duties on export gin.

Orders poured in from every corner of the world, particularly those corners the British had painted pink. Gordon's, for example, records a shipment to a group of Australian miners who sent their payment in advance – in gold dust. The reputation of English gin began to travel the world. One important spin-off was that 'English gin' became accepted as a guarantee of quality, much as is French brandy and Russian caviare.

Opposite
William Ewart Gladstone (1809–98) was Prime Minister four times. He blamed the ending of his first term of office on anti-prohibitionists who had opposed his Government's attempts to control the sale of alcohol.

GIN AND THE BRITISH EMPIRE

Gin's image was greatly enhanced by the prestige of Britain's Empire and the gin-drinking habits of its servants. In the 19th century, while Navy other ranks drank the traditional rum, gin became the drink of officers. (The same had been true a century earlier on Dutch ships where the officers drank jenever, the lower orders rum.) Mixing gin with the daily dose of Angostura bitters, taken to prevent stomach disorders, gave birth to the classic Navy drink, the pink gin. The connection between gin and the Navy remains in the 'gin pennant', the green and white flag traditionally run up as an invitation to board.

Gin was also the drink of choice of the administrators and officer classes throughout the Colonies. When they finally came home to the tranquillity of Cheltenham and Tunbridge Wells, they brought the taste for gin with them. And, if gin was good enough for Rear Vice Admiral (rtd) Jenkins, it must be all right for the hoi polloi.

UPWARDLY MOBILE

A further sign of social acceptance was that in the 1890s distillers began to sell gin in bottles in response to the growing demand from the off licence trade. Until then it had been sold in

Above

The British in India were the first to make the connection between gin and tonic water when they livened-up their daily anti-malarial with a dash of the London Dry.

barrels to the retailers, who would bottle it themselves for customers to take home. The first gin bottles were dark green and of an elongated heart shape, direct copies of Dutch jenever bottles. Later bottles were made of clear glass, a development which was a result of the export trade and consumers' mistrust of goods that had travelled long distances. (This distinction is still to be seen in Gordon's bottling practices where domestic gin is sold in dark green bottles and export gin in clear.) With bottling came sophisticated labelling and advertising, all of which promoted gin as a quality product.

Opposite
The difference is clear – Gordon's export gin is instantly distinguished from the green of its home sales product.

THE FIRST COCKTAILS

Equally important to gin's social status was the influx into Europe of rich, sophisticated Americans undertaking their version of the Grand Tour, who sometimes shipped back the bits of European heritage they really liked. As they wandered Europe in search of culture, they spread the fashion for cocktails – the heavily sweetened mixed drinks that had become all the rage at home.

There has been much debate about the etymology of the word cocktail and a variety of explanations: one describes it as coming from the Aztec princess *Xochitl*; another from the description of a horse of mixed breeds. However,

Opposite and below

Gordon's takes on the cocktail

one of the most likely explanations is that it derives from the French word *coquetel*, a mixed drink. Certainly cocktails, that is mixed drinks, were referred to as far back as 1806 when a cocktail was cynically described as 'an excellent electioneering potion'. By the mid-1850s, in the United States cocktails were considered as a morning 'eye opener', and a 'Kentucky breakfast' was 'three cocktails and a chaw of terbacker'. Clearly people then were made of sterner stuff.

The first US-produced dry gin was made by Fleischmann's in Ohio from about 1870 and dry gin and Old Tom sweet gin co-existed happily at this stage. The main reason why both featured so prominently in cocktail recipes was that they were drinks which were at their best when mixed with other ingredients, which is indeed true of all gin. Gin is not a solo performer, a drink to be sipped and savoured neat as, say, malt whisky and brandy are: it is rather the conductor of the orchestra.

Cocktails caught on. Bar manuals for home mixers rather than professional barkeepers appeared. In 1862 Professor Jerry Thomas, a well-known American bartender, published *The Bar-Tender's Guide and Bon Vivant's Companion*, with recipes for cocktails, many of which were based on gin. He toured Europe with his own travelling bar and met with great success. Harry Johnson's *Bartender's Manual, or How to Mix Drinks of the Present Style* followed in 1882. It also contained many gin-based recipes and became another best seller. By 1892 we find proprietary ready-mixed cocktails on the market. One of the first – a mix of gin and red vermouth, a sort of super sweet Martini – was made by Heublein's of Hartford, Connecticut.

In the 1860s long-established grand hotels and restaurants in most European capitals opened cocktail bars to cater for American travellers. The first American bar serving cocktails in England

She's glad he said Gordon's...

Glad because she knows how much nicer her gin-and-bitter lemon is – when it's a Gordon's-and-bitter lemon! Glad, too, because he's remembered she prefers Gordon's. Most people do. For cool, refreshing Gordon's tastes delightful, mixes perfectly, has been known and trusted for nearly 200 years. It's best to give *our* friends Gordon's – clearly today's most popular gin.

more people ask for

Gordon's

than any other gin

51

Opposite

The enormous variety of gin-based drinks spawned by US cocktail culture increased both the sales and the reputation of the London Dry style.

opened in 1868 behind the Bank of England. Some saw the new trend as colonial vulgarity: Londoners Henry Porter and George Roberts recorded their disgust in 1863: 'For the sensation drinks which have lately travelled across the Atlantic we have no friendly feeling…we will pass the American Bar…and express our gratification at the slight success which "Pick-me-up", and "Corpse Reviver" have had in this country'.

They were not altogether right though, because many of the more-understated cups, punches, toddies, flips, fizzes and slings of Victorian England qualify as cocktails. A large proportion of these used the new dry gin as their base and established it as a fashionable and everyday drink, a trend confirmed when the redoubtable Mrs Beeton published recipes for mint julep and gin sling in her famous *Book of Household Management.*

Throughout their long history cocktails have gone in and out of the fashion. This first wave was very much an American phenomenon. It took a new century and the disaster of Prohibition to make the cocktail, especially the gin cocktail, truly international.

Drinks never taste thin with Gordon's Gin

Gordon's Gin has Liqueur Quality and High Proof, 94.4. That means richer flavor...velvety smoothness...drinks that never taste thin. Obey your sense of discrimination...always ask for Gordon's...you'll be amazed at the finer, richer, smoother taste of your gin drinks.

Gordon's Gin

100% NEUTRAL SPIRITS DISTILLED FROM GRAIN • 94.4 PROOF

GIN IN THE 20TH CENTURY

Opposite
Never had being
bad been so good
– ironically,
Prohibition in
America
produced a
burgeoning
drinking culture
that was soon to
cross the pond.

At the turn of the century two events had a major impact on gin drinking.

First, the dreaded phylloxera struck, an aphid infestation that wiped out most of Europe's vineyards, making brandy almost unobtainable. Middle-class spirits drinkers turned to whisky and began to drink gin, and many remained faithful to gin even when brandy reappeared.

Second, in 1898 there was a large-scale reorganisation of the industry. Gordon's and Tanqueray joined forces to become the major presence in the English distilling industry. Their combined economic power was enormous and, through rationalisation of their production processes and the beginnings of a marketing strategy, they positioned gin as an international drink.

PROHIBITION IN AMERICA

Given the social conditions it is easy to understand why Prohibition was attempted – and equally easy to understand why it failed. America in the 19th century had been dominated

by alcohol drinking. The reaction against was severe: by 1834 there were 1 million members of temperance societies out of a population of 13 million.

However, it wasn't about numbers. The anti-alcohol crusade was a long, slow battle that the reformers realised could be won only by a national ban, ratified by all the states. Through a mixture of blackmail, bribery and clever co-ordination of all the anti-alcohol elements, their efforts to turn America dry eventually paid off. In 1917 Congress adopted the 18th Amendment, which was made law on 17 January 1920 when the Volstead Act came into force. Under the terms of the Act, it became a crime to manu-facture or sell any beverage containing more than 0.5 per cent alcohol (the weakest alcoholic drink contains about 2.5 per cent alcohol).

Its immediate results were utterly predictable – a duplication of the Gin Craze of 18th-century London when an entire population turned to distilling and drinking. A popular song of the time tells it like it was:

Mother makes brandy from cherries
Pop distils whisky and gin;
Sister sells wine from the grapes on our vine –
Good grief how the money rolls in!

So great were the rewards to be gained from illicit alcohol manufacture and smuggling, that gangsters like Al Capone and Dutch Schultz quickly moved in. Their activities led to organised crime on a scale that had never been seen before. Bath-tub gin was the big seller – a deadly combination of industrial alcohol, glycerine and juniper oil – so-called not because it was made in the bath-tub but because it was made in such tall jugs and pots that the only way to add water was from the bath tap. To conceal its often terrible taste and to make it go further, fruit juices, other spirits and bitters were added and a whole host of new cocktails was invented.

The effect of Prohibition on the English gin industry was, perversely, exactly the opposite of what had been anticipated. Prohibition terrified English distillers, who feared for their valuable export trade. Some, including Gordon's, had had to mothball plans for production in the USA. However, as private stocks of liquor ran out and America entered the era of the home brew, the reputation of English gin soared. In 1924 over 4,000 people died from the effects of drinking bad alcohol and people began to be prepared to pay whatever it cost for good-quality spirits. So, it's hardly surprising that, throughout Prohibition, London distilleries continued to export large amounts (an official estimate of 40 million dollars' worth) to different destinations – Canada, the West Indies and tiny islands just off America's eastern seaboard. One offshore

Below
The effect of Prohibition on the export market was exactly the opposite of what the English distillers had feared. Offshore sales boomed once private stocks ran out.

company received an order for a large consignment of gin, cash in advance, specifying that the consignment be packaged in such a way that it could float. With serious money and human greed involved, not even the regular deployment of twenty US Navy destroyers could end the smuggling.

By 1930 it was obvious that Prohibition was unenforceable. America moved deeper into economic depression and the only people profiting from Prohibition were the gangsters. The anti-prohibition movement swung into action led chiefly by prominent women who were outraged by the way ordinary people had been transformed into criminals by 'The Noble Experiment'. They were extremely effective and on 5 December 1933 Prohibition came to an end.

But one lasting benefit was that America learned that drink was a part of civilised society and, like everything else in life, only the best was good enough. Certainly the prestige of and demand for London Dry gin had never been higher.

COCKTAILS AND COMPANY

The modern cocktail hour was born during the years between the wars, a time of tremendous social upheaval when many old social customs disappeared. For the young and fashionable, one immediate change was that dressing for formal

dinners was out. Suddenly those crucial evening hours between 6 and 8 were a social vacuum, which no one quite knew how to fill. Early-evening gatherings at which cocktails were served were already in vogue in America, where grand hotels had transformed the English custom of five o'clock tea into the cocktail hour. (The first American cocktail shakers imitated teapots and cocktail hours were called teas until well into the 1930s.) Like everything American at the time, the fashion spread throughout Europe.

Reliable sources state that the cocktail party was introduced to London in the late 1920s by an American-born hostess called Madame Alfredo de Peña. Certainly from this time there is evidence of a growing cocktail culture influencing fashion, accessories, a host of gadgetry, literature, popular music and film. According to Alec Waugh, brother of Evelyn (who chronicled the Bright Young Things of the cocktail age in such novels as *Vile Bodies* and *Decline and Fall*) and himself a writer, the first cocktails were versions of rum swizzles. Soon, the mixed-up, disaffected generations of the twenties and thirties were drinking mixed-up drinks based on gin.

Opposite

Gin became the perfect early evening mellower for the fast-set between the wars.

GIN POST-WAR

Gin-based cocktails continued to be fashionable throughout the thirties and, although gin production suffered as a result of the restrictions imposed during the Second World War, it was a relatively easy matter to get it going again. Gin boomed post-war well into the 1950s. Only with the remarkable rise of vodka in the fifties and early sixties did gin begin to lose momentum and market share. It was perceived as old hat and middle-aged, the drink of the Home Counties, bridge-playing set – definitely uncool. Solving this image problem was no simple matter but, through a combination of the traditional brands' investment in promoting gin generically and the emergence of new, high-strength, high-flavour brands, gin has made a remarkable comeback. It has become, once again, the drink of the fashionable.

MAKING GIN

Opposite
The purity of
gin is evident in
both its crystal
clear appearance
and its clean
aromatic taste.

Gin is a clear, rectified, unaged alcohol, further distilled together with a selection of natural fruit and herb flavourings known as 'botanicals'. Its base is a pure neutral spirit that can in theory be made out of any substance that will ferment – rice, potatoes, cane, wheat or barley for instance. In practice, the best gin is always made from a grain spirit usually derived from a fermentation of maize. Some gin producers use a molasses spirit which, although cheaper to produce, is less good, flatter and has a slightly sweet aftertaste.

Because gin is made from wholly natural ingredients and through a process that is essentially about purifying the alcohol, it contains very few of the less-pure oils or other organic chemicals formed during fermentation or primary distilling, known collectively as the congeners. Congeners are technically impurities but they contribute greatly to flavour. In some malt whiskies and red wines, over four hundred different congeners have been identified: gin generally has an average of three. Research has shown that the hangover is related to the quantity of congeners in alcohol and so gin is the alcoholic drink least likely to cause a hangover.

Opposite
Continuous
distillation at
Greenall's.

First things first. Distillation itself is a simple process. It starts with a fermented liquor containing alcohol. Alcohol's boiling point is 78.3°C whereas water comes to the boil at 100°C. When a fermented liquor is heated, therefore, the alcohol in it will separate and rise in vapour form. This vapour can then be run off, cooled and collected. As it cools, it returns to a liquid form – the spirit, the *aqua vitae* of the ancients.

CONTINUOUS DISTILLATION

The pure spirit that is the base for gin is made through a process of continuous distillation in a still similar to the type allegedly invented in 1830 by Aeneas Coffey, a Dublin Excise Officer. He may

well have been the first to patent the still in Britain but continuous stills seem to have been developed in other locations at around the same time.

The continuous still is essentially a cylindrical column containing a series of perforated plates. Steam is fed into the top and the cold wash, that is the alcohol-bearing liquid, is introduced at the bottom. As they travel across the plates the alcohol in vapour form is separated out. It is then captured in the condenser, where it cools and becomes liquid again.

The advantage of continuous distillation is that the strength of the final spirit can be predetermined. Gin distillers require a neutral spirit at 96 per cent alcohol by volume (abv) and that's exactly what they get. Technically it would be simple enough to redistil this on the spot as there is no need to age gin – but life is never that simple. Under British law, gin distillers are not allowed to produce their neutral spirit at the same location as the rectified spirit, nor can they transport it at a higher proof than 96 per cent abv. So the spirit is

Opposite

Early Gordon's advertising makes the distinction between unsweetened "dry" gin and heavily sweetened "Old Tom" style.

transferred, usually by road in container loads, to the gin distillery to be rectified or redistilled. (For simplicity's sake the phrase 'gin distillery' is used throughout this book. Strictly speaking the place where gin is made is a rectifier.)

Before the spirit is dispatched to the distillery, samples are sent ahead for tasting. The spirit is tested again on arrival to ensure it conforms to the quality standards because, as a still man will tell you, the spirit is the heart of a gin. Much depends on its quality and, equally, on its ability to achieve consistency of the brand.

Nowadays, given the octopus-like nature of the large distilling concerns, most gin distillers will source their grain spirit from sister companies within their own group of businesses. Gordon's and Tanqueray, for example, buy their spirit from UDV's grain whisky plant at Cameronbridge in Scotland. The Greenwich Distillery also provides large quantities of grain spirit for redistillation.

REDISTILLATION

There are two ways of making gin. One is the method called 'cold compounding' where flavourings, often artificial essences, are added and mixed with the spirit, usually molasses spirit. You'll sometimes find compounded gins sold as supermarket own labels and once opened you will recognise them at once by their perfumed, 'room freshener' smell and taste. (The best way

to avoid those gins is to check the label and select only those that say 'distilled gin' or '100 per cent grain spirit' on the bottle.)

The other, indeed the only proper, way of making gin is by redistillation of the base spirit with natural botanicals. Under EU regulations, this is the definition of 'London Dry gin'. The gin must also be colourless and unsweetened. This is what we mean when we talk about a premium gin.

Premium gin is a subtle, complex drink. Each brand has its own unique flavour, often not immediately obvious because of the addition of mixers. (When tasting a new gin, it's worth following the Navy tradition of adding an equal measure of still water as you then get a far better idea of the gin's true character.)

Reputable distillers use only natural ingredients and each distillery will have its own jealously guarded recipe specifying the types and quantities of botanicals used.

STILLS

Knowledgeable gin distillers will tell you that the design of the pot-still is crucially important as its shape will influence the rate at which the spirit vaporises. This in turn affects the flavour of the gin. Most gin stills are copper pot stills with high 'swan' necks to help extract the higher, more fragrant elements of the spirit. At many distilleries original pot-stills are carefully preserved and copied. Gordon's has one, called Old Tom, that has been used for over 200 years and is the model for the other stills built since. These still have interceptors at the top to retain the botanicals and prevent them being drawn into the head of the still. At the Blackfriars distillery in Plymouth, the oldest working gin distillery in the country, the 155-year-old still has a shorter neck than normal and a steeper curve in the lie pipe. Why? Because that's the way it's always been and because the distillers believe that this design contributes to Plymouth Gin's full-bodied character.

Opposite
The original Gordon's gin still, now over 200 years old, on which all subsequent Gordon's stills have been modelled.

Below
A specially adapted Carterhead still used in the now rare 'racking' method of distillation.

ADDING THE BOTANICALS

Over 120 botanicals, some of which are described later in this chapter, can be found in gin although most gins use no more than seven or eight. In most botanical mixes there will generally be about 40 per cent juniper, 40 per cent coriander and 10 per cent angelica. It is the proportion of other botanicals that differentiates one brand from another. Distillers commonly use lemon peel, orange peel, angelica, cassia bark and orris root, others add calamus root, liquorice, cardamom and cinnamon. A new brand on the market uses ginger and lemon grass, and there is even one extremely good gin that features bergamot and could be described as the Earl Gray of gin. Some gins such as Tanqueray, Plymouth and Polo Club are exceptionally dry, usually because their recipes call for a greater proportion of rooty substances such as liquorice and angelica. Others, like Beefeater, will be quite distinctly citric because they contain larger amounts of orange or lemon peel.

Production methods depend very much on the original recipe of the brand. At many distilleries, UDV's for example where Gordon's, Tanqueray and Booth's are made, the botanicals are added to neutral spirit and purified water in a traditional copper pot still and steam heat is gently applied until boiling temperature is reached. Gordon's uses the two-shot method whereby the still is charged with botanicals at several times the strength of the recipe and neutral alcohol is added after distillation to restore the original proportions of the recipe.

Beefeater steeps the botanicals in a pot still with the base spirit for 24 hours before distilling. This means the stills can be run only once every two days but the company's Desmond Payne believes that this slower process allows for a gentler extraction of flavour from the botanicals before distillation and makes for a more complex drink.

Greenall's Distillery in Warrington uses specially adapted Carterhead stills for the now rare 'racking' method when making Bombay Sapphire and Bombay Dry (see illustration p.72). Neutral grain alcohol alone at 192 proof is put into a traditional pot still with a long rectifying column attached. The still's temperature is maintained at a steady 82°C so that the alcohol reaches boiling point but not the water. The botanicals are placed in a copper container at the furthest point of the still's neck. Inside is a copper basket with seven smaller lift-out mesh baskets. Botanicals in powder form, such as almond, orris and nutmeg, are placed in the central basket and the others distributed evenly around the other six baskets. By the racking method the spirit meets the botanicals in vapour form and passes slowly through the baskets, picking up the different flavours and aromas. The effect is one of 'steaming' rather than the more traditional 'boiling' process.

THE UNIQUE BOMBAY SAPPHIRE DISTILLATION PROCESS

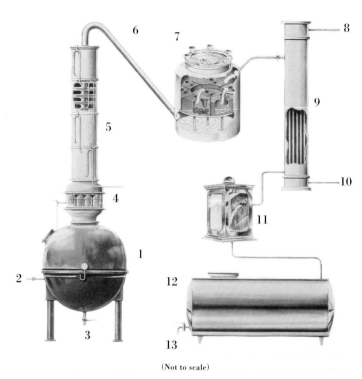

(Not to scale)

1. Carterhead still
2. Steam inlet
3. Steam outlet
4. Feints chamber
5. Rectifying column

6. Vapour pipe
7. Copper botanicals basket
8. Water outlet
9. Water condenser
10. Water inlet

11. Spirit safe
12. Receiving tank
13. Bottling line feed

A distillation takes about 7–8 hours to complete. As the mix of alcohol and botanicals goes through the still, the flavour of each botanical peaks at different times. Orange and lemon peel are usually the first to emerge, quickly followed by juniper and coriander. Stand at the spirit safe during a run and you will undergo various different olfactory sensations. It can be a disconcerting experience, especially if you are next to a still making Tanqueray and suddenly feel yourself, as I did, immersed in a jar of liquorice allsorts.

Opposite

The Bombay Sapphire distillation process.

MAKING THE CUT

The first and last parts of the run through the still are discarded because they contain unwanted flavours – oily or off, too strong, too weak. Judging the right moment to make the 'middle cut', as it is called, is critical. Once the distillation begins, therefore, the spirit is constantly tested by the still men. Only when they are satisfied that it has achieved the consistent flavours and characteristics of the brand is the spirit collected in the spirit receiver while the 'feints' and 'forenotes' are diverted into another receptacle to be distilled again.

No two distillers will cut at exactly the same time or at exactly the same strength. The decision is part of the recipe and remains a trade secret. Some gins, however, are noticeably heavier, with more rooty, more robust aromas. This is partly because they contain larger proportions of rooty substances and partly, one supposes, because they will have been left to run longer to pick up the heavier elements of the spirit. Others are lighter in taste with more pronounced citric tones and will probably have been cut at a higher strength at an earlier point in the run.

REDUCTION TO BOTTLING STRENGTH

Once distillation is complete the final stage is to reduce the gin to its bottling strength by adding water. In European law the alcoholic content of gin must be at least 37.5 per cent abv (equivalent to 75 proof in North America). In practice gins vary between this minimum and up to 55 per cent abv, with experts agreeing that most gins taste best at between 40 and 43 per cent. The reason given is that the bands of flavour within gin are held by the alcoholic content of the spirit; reduce the alcoholic content and, even without the addition of mixers, some of the flavours and aromas present, particularly those derived from the more volatile citric elements, will disappear. Since Gordon's dropped the strength of its brand from 40 per cent to 37.5 per cent abv there has been a

marked change in flavour, easily detected by comparing Gordon's at 37.5 per cent with export strength Gordon's at 40 per cent abv.

A word, too, about water. It is no accident that the 18th-century distillers made sure that their distilleries were located in those parts of London which were noted for the purity of their water. Water is an alarmingly high percentage of a bottle of gin so the water used in the distilling process and to reduce the final spirit must be exceptionally pure. Distillers use filtered, de-mineralised water which is neutral and analytically pure and, although most would hesitate to claim mystical properties for their water, it is recognised that the quality of the water has a significant part to play in the final quality of the gin.

Below
A Gordon's bottling factory. Once distillation is complete, gin is diluted back to a drinkable strength before it is packaged for sale.

THE BOTANICALS

Opposite
A botanical
drawing of the
angelica plant.

As soon as you walk into the room where the botanicals are stored in any distillery, you are instantly aware of how much of a debt today's drinks' cabinets owe to yesterday's medicine chests. The rich melange of aromas – sweet, spicy, fragrant, sharp, fruity – is gloriously unsettling. When considering the vast array of exotic ingredients, one is reminded too that gin is the national drink of two countries that, in their heyday, were the foremost trading nations in the world. The Dutch and the English between them dominated the spice trade for centuries; indeed it was the cause of much strife between them, partially resolved only when England swapped the Banda Islands, the principal source of nutmeg in the 17th century, for an unimportant outpost of the Dutch in America, Manhattan Island.

ALMOND

The almond tree is closely related to the peach tree and grows everywhere in southern Europe. There are two types of almond – the familiar sweet almond and the bitter almond used in gin. Bitter almonds are as hard and inedible as peach kernels and must be ground before use to release their oil.

ANGELICA BACCIFERA

ANGELICA ROOT

Angelica originated in Iceland, Greenland and northern Russia but is now found throughout Europe. Its sweetening properties are much

valued in the kitchen and the root is used in traditional Chinese medicine. It is also reputed to guard against witchcraft – perhaps not strictly necessary at the local pub, but you never know. The great benefit of angelica in a gin recipe is that it helps to 'fix' the flavours of the other aromatics.

CARDAMOM

These small pods contain numerous tiny black seeds which have a warm, spicy, aromatic flavour. The best cardamom comes from Sri Lanka and the seeds of green cardamom pods are considered to be more delicately flavoured than black pods. In India the seeds of green cardamom are highly prized for their digestive properties and are often served raw after meals to sweeten the breath and aid digestion. Cardamom pods are usually lightly crushed before use to allow their full flavour to emerge.

CASSIA BARK

In China cassia is considered one of the six great spices. Cassia oil derives from the bark of cinnamon-like trees. It resembles cinnamon in flavour but is stronger and more bitter. It is often used in skin care and at one time cassia extracts were mixed with almond oil to make Macassar oil – a popular Victorian hair oil for men that produced an urgent requirement for antimacassars, those little panels of crocheted fabric that your great aunt draped over the backs of her chairs. Cassia smells and tastes very like some chewing gums.

Below
Coriander seeds.

Opposite
Angelica root.

CORIANDER

Coriander seeds are the second most commonly used botanical and have formed part of the botanicals mix for centuries. If coriander seems an exotic ingredient for 18th-century English distillers, it should be remembered that it was grown commercially in southern England long before the days of global warming. Coriander seeds look like mini

rugby balls and have a fresh, slightly spicy, sage and lemon flavour. Most distillers source their

Opposite
Botanical
drawings of the
flora of the
Juniper.

coriander from southern Europe, though spicier gins such as Bombay Dry and Bombay Sapphire use the more pungent coriander from Morocco.

CUBEB BERRIES

A member of the pepper family, the small reddish-brown cubebs come from Java. They have a spicy, peppery aroma and contribute a flavour of lemon and pine.

GRAINS OF PARADISE

These glamorously named berries are imported from West Africa where they grow profusely. They look like tiny dark brown nuts and have a peppery taste with hints of lavender and camphor.

GINGER

Ginger is an aromatic root from the jungles of south-east Asia. Its distinctive smell and fiery taste make it a popular ingredient in most Asian cuisines. Ginger is much used in traditional Chinese medicine and has a reputation as an aphrodisiac and a purifier of the blood.

JUNIPER

A small, prickly, coniferous evergreen shrub, juniperus communis grows profusely throughout Europe. The best juniper berries are from Umbrian hilltops and from above the tree line in the former Yugoslavia. The berries take three

years to ripen so that green and riper blue berries are found on the same plant. Traditionally they are harvested by knocking the branches of each shrub with a stick.

Distilleries ensure that the juniper they use is of the highest quality and will test samples – in the case of Gordon's over 200 different ones – from each year's harvest before they purchase the year's supply. On arrival at the distillery, the juniper berries are stored in hessian sacks in cool, dry conditions for anything up two years until just before they turn black, when their aromatic oil is at its richest. During this time the master distiller regularly samples the berries to decide which batches are ready. Different gins use different proportions of juniper in their recipes but its taste is instantly recognisable – bittersweet and oily, with hints of pine, lavender and camphor – the taste of the mountains. Medicinally, oil of juniper is given as a diuretic for kidney and bladder infections and is also used in the treatment of indigestion and flatulence.

Opposite
Juniper berries
ripened and
ready for use.

LEMON PEEL

Lemon oil is refreshing and invigorating, with many ancient medicinal applications. Lemon peel contributes a fresh, citrus flavour to gin, enhancing its dryness.

LIQUORICE

The liquorice plant is native to south-eastern Europe and the Middle East. Its roots descend below ground for about 1 metre, sending out the horizontal rhizomes that are used as flavouring. The bitter-sweet liquorice root has been enjoyed as a natural confection for thousands of years and is also widely used in the treatment of coughs and bronchitis.

NUTMEG

Nutmeg is widely used in Western and Eastern cooking, its warm, sweet flavour with a slightly bitter undertone blending well with other spices. Its uses are extremely varied. In large quantities it is hallucinogenic.

ORANGE PEEL

Dried orange peel releases a sweet oil that is mildly sedative and often used as an anti-depressant. Some brands use bitter orange, others sweet orange.

ORRIS ROOT

Orris is the fragrant root of the iris plant. It smells of sweet violets and is used in talcum powder and potpourri mixes. The orris used in distilling comes mainly from irises grown in southern France and Italy. Once the plants are 3–4 years old, they are lifted, dried and kept for two years, during which time their fragrance increases. Orris root helps to bind together all the flavours of the botanicals.

MAKING DUTCH JENEVER

In the history of international spirits, Schiedam, just outside Rotterdam, plays as significant a role as the Scottish Highlands or the Cognac region. In fact when gin arrived in England it was equally commonly known as Schiedam or Hollands. By 1880, the heyday of Dutch jenever production, there were 392 distilleries in this relatively small place and a thriving mono-economy of coopers, brass and cork factories, malt houses, yeast makers and glass works. Surrounding the town, twenty enormous windmills, the largest in the world, ground the grain to feed the stills.

Because the Dutch were the dominant seafaring nation, trade in jenever was huge. From 1650, the Dutch Golden Age, onwards, wherever the Dutch went they took jenever with them and it gained an international dominance never again achieved by any other type of alcoholic drink. By 1792 the Dutch were exporting 4.2 million gallons of jenever annually. Jenever is still Holland's national drink, and the Dutch have more than 750 nicknames for it.

In recent times, jenever has suffered from many of the social stigmas that characterise traditional spirits in the UK and its consumption is now only about half that of twenty years ago. It's considered a drink for the older generation, drunk only on traditional occasions, a drink

Above
*Enormous
windmills grind
the grain to feed
the stills of the
Dutch jenever
distilleries.*

people drink to get drunk. If one ignores this bad press one finds that jenever is a characterful and versatile drink with its own particular charm.

Nowadays even the most modern Dutch distillery resembles nothing so much as a giant kitchen and, as soon as you walk in, you smell the distinctive yeasty smell that causes the Dutch to call their national drink 'liquid bread'.

Like English gin, Dutch jenever is made in two stages: unlike English gin, both are carried out at the same distillery. First the half product (the base spirit) is made. It is either a molasses or grain spirit, made in a column still and then blended with *moutwijn* (maltwine). Maltwine is a malted grain spirit made from a mixture of rye, malted barley and wheat and its fiery taste is what gives jenever its distinctive character. Each style of jenever contains a different percentage of maltwine.

Traditionally the process of making maltwine starts with a mash of flour and water in giant tubs to which yeast is added. Once fermentation is complete, the liquid is then distilled three times in pot stills, increasing in alcohol content from 12 per cent through 24 per cent and finally to 47 per cent.

Depending on which style of jenever is being made, there are different methods of combining the base spirit with the botanicals. Some distillers redistil a percentage of the last distillation of maltwine with the botanicals and blend it with the base spirit to allow the flavours to settle. Others will combine a percentage of maltwine with a grain or molasses spirit and redistil the whole with the botanicals. Each distillery has its own way of doing things, based on tradition and how it wants its products to taste. Whatever method is used, the final stage of jenever

Extra oude belegen
Corenwyn®
gestookt door
Erven Lucas Bols
opgericht te Amsterdam
in den jare 1575
Gerijpt op fust

e 1 l   38% vol

Corenwyn®
om het jarenlange rijpingsproces op fust slechts in beperkte
mate beïnvloedt. Het volgnummer en de ongeschonden sluiting
garanderen U de originele Corenwyn, gestookt volgens
zeer oud recept door *Erven Lucas Bols*
NRBR DD
№ 473276   Netkoud serveren

production is usually a reduction of the spirit to 35 per cent abv.

There are three basic styles of jenever – *oude* (old), *jonge* (young) and *korenwijn* (cask aged) – and by law each contains different minimum percentages of malt-wine, botanicals, sugar and other ingredients. In this case the terms *oude* and *jonge* are misleading as one tends to think of them as terms applied to aged and unaged products – think rather of 'old style' and 'new style'.

Oude jenever is the traditional jenever – straw-coloured, sweetened and very aromatic with a strong juniper flavour. A greater range of botanicals is used in making it – Bols' oude, for example, contains aloe and myrrh. Oude jenever must have at least 15 per cent maltwine, which gives it a flavour similar to the taste of 18th-century English gins. Different brands have higher percentages of maltwine: Schermers Wijnkopers makes a jenever with 60 per cent maltwine. Sometimes oude jenever is aged, some-times it isn't.

Jonge jenever is the most commonly drunk jenever. It was developed in the 1950s in response to consumers' demands for a lighter-flavoured drink that could be mixed more easily. It consists of neutral alcohol, which is either grain or molasses, only about 5 per cent maltwine and a small amount of juniper and botanicals. It is colourless, hardly sweetened, very light on the palate and crisp, particularly when drunk ice-cold as is the Dutch custom.

Opposite
A high proportion of maltwine and ageing in wood are what give korenwijn its distinctive malty, fiery taste.

Below
The trademark Bols clay bottles freshly fired in the kiln.

89

Opposite

Barrels for jenever and maltwine were made from oak with iron hoops. It was a skillful job giving employment to many in Schiedam.

Korenwijn is Holland's answer to malt whisky, an attempt by the Dutch distilling industry to create a truly premium heritage product. It contains a minimum of 51 per cent maltwine, which results in a very pronounced malty, full-bodied character. Different brands use different recipes and combinations of botanicals often adding angelica and St. John's Wort. Some redistil for a fourth time, others add a juniper concentrate and leave it to marry with the spirit. Bols produces its "Corenwyn" by redistilling for a fourth time passing the vapour over juniper berries. Korenwijn, like malt whisky, is aged in wood, for anything from one to many years.

Korenwijn is served cold in tulip shaped glasses. In Schiedam the glasses are brought to the table minus their bases with the stems embedded in a wooden block, an echo of the days when distilleries stopped every hour on the hour for the jenever ration. The distillery head would give the toast 'to heaven' and hand around a glass like this so that the men could down their drams in one and get straight back to work.

Modern jenever and London Dry gin parted company some time ago and today the two taste quite different. Even jonge jenever, the most neutral of the jenever styles, is far more fiery than gin and, in some brands, one can barely taste juniper or botanicals. At the other end of the taste scale, korenwijn's rich, complex flavours are reminiscent of aged whiskies and brandies.

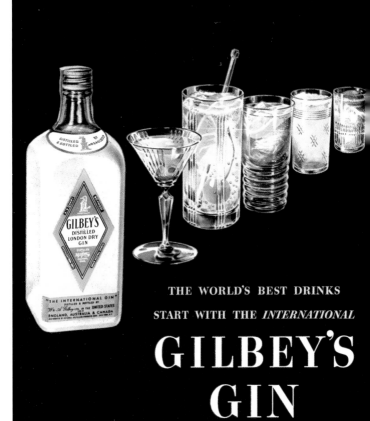

THE WORLD'S BEST DRINKS

START WITH THE *INTERNATIONAL*

GILBEY'S
GIN

CHAPTER FIVE

BRAND DIRECTORY

There are literally thousands of gin brands worldwide. Many are of indifferent or poor quality and are of no interest to the serious gin drinker. This directory confines itself to discussion of classic brands – those that belong to the great distilling houses, newcomers adhering to the tradition of quality, and interesting styles of gin from around the world.

The premium styles of London Dry gin are now so international that whichever country and whatever bar in the world you are in, there will probably be a bottle of a brand mentioned here.

Opposite
Gilbey's advertising from the 40s focuses on the distinctive frosted bottle.

THE GREAT HOUSES

BEEFEATER

James Burroughs was a trained pharmacist who as a young man had travelled widely in the United States and seen the commercial opportunities of producing a superior quality gin. In 1863 he founded the company that produces Beefeater gin. By 1900 the Burroughs company was already exporting to Montreal. During the 1950s, Eric Burroughs concentrated on export markets, particularly that to America.

He capitalised on the mania for British products caused by the interest in the coronation of Queen Elizabeth II and made the 'beefeater' element of the branding more prominent. In 1963 Beefeater was the largest export brand in the British Isles and is still the number two imported gin in the States. The company remained in the control of the Burroughs family until it was acquired by Whitbread in 1987. James Burroughs is now part of Allied-Domecq.

Beefeater is the only London Dry gin actually made in London. It's a dry, complex gin whose citric notes are balanced with hints of caramel. James Burroughs's original recipe is known to contain juniper, coriander, bitter orange peel and angelica root and seed redistilled with a 90 per cent wheat and 10 per cent malt grain spirit. The botanicals are steeped prior to distillation (see pages 70–71) and the final spirit is reduced to 40 per cent abv.

A new product, Beefeater Crown Jewel, is produced solely for the duty-free market. It is Beefeater with knobs on – triple distilled, citrus nose, exceptionally dry and clean and, at 50 per cent abv, exceptionally strong.

BOOTH'S

A document of 1569 refers to the Booth family's involvement in the wine trade. One can presume that they also distilled gin, as most wine merchants did then, although there is no official record until the listing of Philip Booth & Company Distillers of Clerkenwell in the 1778 Directory of Merchants, which makes Booth's and its sister brand Boord's among the oldest gin brands still in existence.

In the following century Sir Felix Booth expanded the business and turned it into the largest distilling company in England. In 1829 he anonymously funded Captain John Ross's unsuccessful expedition to map the elusive North

West Passage, though the true position of the magnetic North Pole was located. In his wanderings around Antarctica, perhaps sustained by copious amounts of Booth's gin, Ross named many of the areas he mapped after his patron. That's why you will find Boothia Peninsula, Felix Harbour, Cape Felix and the Gulf of Boothia in northern Canada.

Booth's was owned by the family until 1896 when, on the death of the last male Booth, it became a limited company. During the 1920s and 1930s Booth's expanded and diversified, acquiring more than twelve different spirits companies including Boord's, an equally venerable brand. Booth's became the premium English gin brand. The company made two London Dry style gins – Booth's Finest and Booth's High and Dry. To promote them, Booth's published *An Anthology of Cocktails* in the thirties, which featured the cocktail choices and photographs of society figures and well-known characters such as Ivor Novello and Lady Oxford. It was an instant hit, for both cocktails and Booth's gin.

Booth's Finest was distinguished by its very slightly golden colour, the result of being stored in sherry casks. Unfortunately in later years, when advertising and marketing for gin began to focus on cleanness and purity, the reputation of this gin suffered for this reason. After the war the company targeted Booth's High and Dry, a very light, dry gin ideal for cocktails, at the American market in order to compete with Tanqueray. It never achieved this and both Booth's brands went into a steady slow decline from which they never fully recovered.

Booth's and Boord's joined forces with DCL in 1927 and are now owned by Diageo. A decision was made to discontinue production of Booth's Finest, but High and Dry is still in production. It is a light, crisp, spicy style of gin with a molasses base, which gives it a more highly flavoured and sweeter taste. Boord's is also still made but now exclusively for Pimms No 1, a not totally undignified fate for a once great brand.

BURNETT'S WHITE SATIN

Sir Robert Burnett joined the company that bears his name in 1770. He was clearly an entrepreneur of the first order because the quest to establish a quality London gin was only the first step in a long and successful career. He became Sheriff of London in 1794 and was knighted the following year.

Burnett's White Satin is a classic-style London Dry gin in that it is distilled with botanicals in the traditional way. Because it uses a molasses base spirit, the flavour of the botanicals is not as clear and defined as it might be. Unfortunately, too, White Satin is one of the gins that followed Gordon's example in dropping its abv to 37.5 per cent, to the detriment of its flavour. To compensate they have launched Burnett's Crown Select, a higher-strength brand. Since 1963, the Burnett's name has been owned by Seagram UK Ltd.

CORK DRY

Cork Dry is the biggest-selling gin in the Irish Republic. It was first made at the Old Watercourse distillery established near Cork in 1793. Nowadays it is made at the Middleton Distilleries by Irish distillers and bottled at 38 per cent with an export version at 43 per cent abv. Cork Dry is triple-distilled dry gin with a malty and pleasantly grainy taste. It is sweeter than UK-produced dry gins because it uses more tangy citrus fruits and is not as strongly juniper flavoured. Its sherbet, fruity flavours make it mellow, very drinkable and somehow very Irish.

GILBEY'S

Walter and Alfred Gilbey were the sons of a Bishop's Stortford coach operator. Returning to London in 1857 from active duty in the Crimean War, the two brothers set up a wine business in Soho, importing fine wines from the Colonies to cater to the needs of the new, prosperous middle class. By 1867 they had done so well they were able to move their premises to the famous Pantheon building in Oxford Street. At about the same time, realising that gin was also becoming middle class, they started producing gin at their Camden Town distillery.

The Gilbeys soon diversified, acquiring several whisky distilleries in Scotland and an impressive portfolio of products including Croft port. Success was rapid. By the 1920s Gilbey's had gin distilleries operating in Australia and Canada. During Prohibition, the Gilbey's empire flourished and the Pantheon offices regularly dispatched consignments of gin for shipment to Antwerp and Hamburg. From there they were shipped to just outside the 12-mile limit and then into the States for customers who paid cash.

Above
Sir Walter Gilbey
was a founder
member of the
distinguished
Gilbey brand.

So popular was Gilbey's gin during Prohibition that it was widely counterfeited. To prevent this special frosted bottles were introduced, the company reverting to the original clear glass style only in 1975. By this time Gilbey's had distilleries in New Zealand, Uruguay, Namibia, East Africa, Swaziland, Mauritius and Mozambique.

Gilbey's is considered to be one of the biggest-selling brands in the world. Ninety per cent of its production goes to feed the insatiable Filipino appetite for gin (see page 145). The Gilbey's brand is now owned by Diageo and has been reduced to 37.5 per cent for the domestic market. To compensate, a premium brand, Antique, has recently been launched. Both are made in the UK at Greenall's Distillery in Warrington.

GORDON'S

Below

Alexander Gordon

Alexander Gordon was an ambitious Scot who founded his distilling business in London in 1769. In 1786 he moved the business to Clerkenwell. On his death in 1823 he was succeeded by his son Charles. His grandson, also Charles, became sole partner in the business in 1847 and sold the firm to John Currie & Co of Bromley by Bow, which produced neutral malt spirit for several distillers. Tanqueray had already received backing from Currie's as a guaranteed outlet for its spirit and, in 1898, Gordon's and Tanqueray were merged to form Tanqueray, Gordon & Co. The move was significant, establishing the two companies as the single most powerful force in English distilling, a position they still occupy.

Gordon's today is the second largest-selling gin in the world with annual sales of over six million cases. Gordon's has opened distilleries in the United States, Canada, South America and Jamaica, where the same ingredients and methods are used as at the UK distillery; samples of the gin produced are even returned to home base for final approval. However, UK-produced Gordon's is considered the most prestigious and is exported to more than 140 countries.

Opposite top

The Gordon's range at the turn of the century.

Opposite bottom

The newly amalgamated Tanqueray and Gordon's London premises.

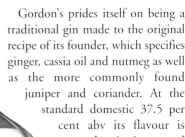

Gordon's prides itself on being a traditional gin made to the original recipe of its founder, which specifies ginger, cassia oil and nutmeg as well as the more commonly found juniper and coriander. At the standard domestic 37.5 per cent abv its flavour is strongly juniper and lemon, with a clean, sharp aftertaste. Perfectly drinkable – until you compare it with export-strength Gordon's, which has been kept at 40 per cent abv. At this strength the flavour is more complex, with an attractive viscosity and pronounced coriander and angelica tones. This is a far better gin and goes a long way towards explaining Gordon's phenomenal success.

G & J GREENALL'S

G & J Greenall's has been producing gin to the same recipes since 1761. In that year Thomas Dakin built a distillery in the centre of Warrington. In 1860 Gilbert and John Greenall began to lease the distillery and by 1870 were able to buy it. The business expanded greatly during the first half of the 1900s and acquired various wine and spirit companies. The company's present distillery, bottling facilities and warehouses were built on land close to the site of the original distillery. The current chairman of the Greenall Group, Lord Daresbury, is a direct descendant of the Greenall family.

The main Greenall's house brand is Original London Dry, which contains eight different botanicals including the less-common cassia bark and ground almonds. It is smooth and very dry with a lingering finish. Original London Dry is a high-strength gin produced at 42 per cent abv for the domestic market. There is a premium version, Greenall's Special London Dry, which has more prominent lemon citrus flavours and is bottled at 48 per cent abv.

Greenall's is also a contract distiller and makes Bombay Dry and Bombay Sapphire as well as other gins such as Richmond and supermarket own labels. Perhaps because of this conflict of interest, Greenall's own brands suffer slightly from lack of exposure – a pity because they are excellent.

PLYMOUTH GIN

The Coates family established a distillery in the old Black Friars Monastery near the Barbican in Plymouth in 1793. It is still there and can justifiably claim to be the oldest working distillery in the country. The building has its own part in history, as the place the Pilgrim Fathers gathered in 1620 before they set off for America in the *Mayflower*.

Plymouth Gin has a long history. It is the only UK gin to have a geographic designation, like an appellation controllée: under EU regulations, Plymouth Gin must be made in Plymouth. One of the

Below

As part of the relaunch of Plymouth gin, the monk on the inside of the bottle's back label has been reintroduced.

107

world's great brands of gin and the one first specified in the dry martini recipe, it suffered 45 years of neglect in the hands of the multinational drinks giants, who never quite knew what to do with it and succeeded only in lowering its strength and cheapening its image. But now Plymouth Gin has been taken over by a private group of investors, which has restored the brand to its original 41.2 per cent strength and, through clever marketing and word of mouth, it has gained enormous exposure. Plymouth is currently the fastest-growing gin brand on the market and is consistently raved about by food and drink experts. A recent deal signed with Seagrams UK ensures that it gets crucial nationwide distribution and will be more generally available.

Traditionally the gin made in Plymouth retained its more aromatic flavour after the introduction of the London Dry style. Modern Plymouth gin has returned to its heritage. It has a subtle, full-bodied flavour and contains a higher than usual proportion of root ingredients, hence its distinctively earthy, rooty tastes. The addition of sweet orange and cardamom imparts a pleasantly fruity, spicy finish. Plymouth still has strong associations with the Navy, which considers an authentic pink gin to be one made with Plymouth.

TANQUERAY

Below
Charles
Tanqueray.

Traditionally described as the 'Rolls Royce of gins', Tanqueray Special Dry is the classic premium gin brand.

Below
Charles Tanqueray.

Charles Tanqueray deliberately located his distillery close to a source of pure spa water in Bloomsbury in 1830 and, ever since, there has been a strong tradition of quality attached to its production. While London Dry gin does not by law have to be distilled in England, all Tanqueray gin is – at the same distillery where Gordon's is made.

One reason for its much-vaunted dryness is the use of cassia bark, cinnamon and liquorice in the botanicals mix. Another is its high strength – Tanqueray has been maintained at 47 per cent abv throughout its history. After the amalgamation of Tanqueray and Gordon's in 1898 and subsequent acquisition by the Distillers Company, Tanqueray lost place to its sister brand. In the 1950s a decision was made to push Tanqueray at the export market, which is not to say that Tanqueray had not enjoyed export success before – almost from the start Tanqueray

Opposite below
Barrels of gin ready for the export market. Tanqueray is now the USA's biggest imported gin.

had been an international drink appreciated by, among others, plantation owners in Jamaica.

Tanqueray is now the United States' biggest imported gin, accounting for over half the bottles sold. It has always had social prestige in American where fans have included Frank Sinatra, Bob Hope and John F Kennedy. Tanqueray still has a particularly English, exclusive, upper-class image, reinforced by the fact that it is more expensive than most other brands. It also looks different.

Opposite
The 'Great Houses' that flourished under the first gin regulations, have retained their leading status due to their own rigorous monitoring of the product.

Tanqueray branding is protected by world-wide patent, as is its bottle. Contrary to some opinions, it was not modelled on the shape of a 19th-century fire hydrant but rather on the design of the cocktail shaker. The 'holdability' factor of the bottle, plus Tanqueray's exceptional dryness, which makes it the ideal gin for cocktails, lies behind its international success. Thankfully, since its relaunch on the home market in the 1990s, Tanqueray is generally available in the UK.

THE NEWCOMERS

Gin's decline in the seventies and eighties was partly caused by the fact that it was seen as an old-fashioned drink and partly by many brands dropping in strength, and hence in flavour, just at the time when, of all the white spirits, gin most needed to attract new audiences. One brand, Bombay Original, gently led gin out of its identity crisis, paving the way for a clutch of new, full-strength, big-flavoured, stylishly presented gins. These new uber gins are deliberately designed to appeal to sophisticated young adult consumers who demand something new and different. Despite the fact that they are sold at premium prices, the newcomers have led the renaissance of gin drinking.

BOMBAY DRY

Not strictly a newcomer since it has been around since the late 1950s, Bombay Dry was launched by an American, Alan Subin. He saw the opportunity to create a new gin to challenge Tanqueray and Beefeater in the United States, and approached the Greenall's distillery in Warrington with a name and a marketing plan, but without a specific taste. Greenall's came up with Bombay Dry – very lemony, dry and spicy with strong coriander and juniper flavours and made by the infusion method (see page 73). Initially Bombay Dry was distilled in Warrington and bottled in Edinburgh. In 1964 it began to be bottled at source and in 1968 Carillon Importers took over its distribution in the USA. Sadly, Bombay Dry is now available only in Spain and the United States. Based on a 100 per cent pure grain spirit and bottled at 40 per cent, it is a delightful gin, its spicy notes blending perfectly with tonic water.

BOMBAY SAPPHIRE

Bombay Sapphire is the marketing triumph of the 1990s. It was developed in 1988 by Michel Roux, president of Carillon, who had launched Absolut vodka on the American market. His idea was to help boost the depressed gin market by creating a speciality gin based on Bombay Dry. Bombay Sapphire has succeeded probably beyond his wildest dreams. In the recent shakeup of the distilling industry both Bombay brands have been taken over by Bacardi Ltd.

Above

The unusual combination of botanicals that together create the unique taste of Bombay Sapphire.

Bombay Sapphire is a premium gin in the same style as Bombay Dry but with something extra. That something is the use of 11 botanicals in the mix and immensely stylish packaging and marketing, which has made it the fastest-growing international gin brand. Bombay Sapphire in its instantly recognisable, translucent blue bottle now symbolises gin for the young and hip. To the traditional flavourings Bombay Sapphire adds a spicier type of coriander from Morocco, orris root, liquorice, cassia bark, almonds, cubeb berries from Java and grains of paradise from West Africa. Like Bombay Dry, it is redistilled in a Carterhead still using the infusion method. The result is a gin with spicy, peppery and fragrant notes.

BURBERRY'S LONDON DRY

Burberry's London Dry gin is made under licence by Burn Stewart Distillers, the third largest independent Scotch whisky company, at their distillery in Doune, Perthshire. It is the sister brand to Burberry's Premium Scotch whisky and was launched in conjunction with the famous fashion and accessory house. The Burberry's logo and distinctive chequered pattern are featured heavily in the branding. Bottled at 40 and 43 per cent, this is a high-quality premium gin made in the traditional way with very strong juniper and citrus flavours. Burberry's is made only for the export market. Burn Stewart also makes a premium brand, Churchill's, for the domestic market.

CADENHEAD'S OLD RAJ

The name of Cadenhead is traditionally associated with specialist bottlings of exceptionally high-strength single malt whiskies and the firm has a loyal clientele of whisky buffs and food gurus. What is less well known is that Cadenhead's produces and bottles gin under its own brand name, Old Raj. Old Raj gin is made in a slightly unusual fashion in that the botanicals are steeped in a mixture of alcohol and water and then distilled separately in a small pot still. The resulting essence is then added to a neutral grain spirit. Old Raj is bottled at 46 and 55 per cent abv. At 46 per cent it is very juniper, spirity and peppery with a slight medicinal taste from the high alcohol content; at 55 per cent it is very aromatic, full and rounded. Both can be highly recommended. Old Raj Gin is also distinctive because it contains a measure of saffron, which gives it a yellowish-green colour.

CITADELLE

One knows that a style trend has been established once the French get in on the act. Citadelle is a new gin brand produced to a centuries-old recipe in Ars in France by Cognac's Garbiel & Andreu. It's distilled with no fewer than 19 botanicals and sold in a distinctive light blue bottle. The use of so many botanicals tends to crowd out the juniper flavour but gives it interesting aromatic, herbal, spicy notes.

DARESBURY'S QUITESSENTIAL DRY

A new super-premium brand that has become an instant classic. Daresbury's Quintessential Dry is named after Lord Daresbury, chairman of the Greenall's Group. It is made at their Warrington distillery and is high-strength at 45 per cent abv and exceptionally clean and dry in flavour, possibly due to the fact that it is distilled five times in all – as an essence with each of the four botanicals and then a fifth time with extra juniper and lime. Unfortunately it is currently available only in the United States, but this may change.

EDINBURGH

The Edinburgh Gin Company is a product of the Martinelli Group, which also produces London Original Dry. It is a tremendous, full-strength gin with strong ginger and lemon flavours. Edinburgh gin, also known as Prince's gin, is the only gin in the world to use Scottish juniper berries, a throwback to the 17th century when Scotland was a major exporter of juniper to the Dutch jenever trade. The company is involved in a joint venture with the Borders Forest Trust to revive the juniper-growing industry in Scotland.

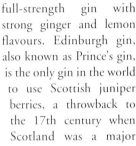

GLOAG'S

Launched in 1996 by Matthew Gloag & Son, makers of Famous Grouse whisky, Gloag's gin is a traditionally produced, double distilled London Dry gin. Eleven botanicals are used in the flavouring mix, including dried sweet orange peel, Indonesian nutmeg and grains of paradise. The botanicals are steeped prior to distilling to release their flavour and the final product is left to marry before bottling at 40 per cent abv. The result is a pleasantly flowery gin with tantalising spice and citrus notes.

KINGSTREE ORIGINAL LONDON DRY

An entirely new brand, Kingstree Original London Dry gin is made to a traditional recipe from 100 per cent grain spirit distilled three times. Sharp and spicy on the nose, probably because of the addition of cubeb berries, it is a classically clean London Dry gin with a pleasant almond finish.

LICHFIELD BRITISH DRY

Lichfield British Dry gin is the result of a partnership between the photographer Lord Lichfield and William Grant & Sons, distillers of Glenfiddich malt whisky. Launched in 1995, it is made to an original recipe and is triple-distilled using eight botanicals including the less common cassia bark, orris root and almonds. Premium strength Lichfield, at 40 per cent abv, is a classically English-style gin – crisp, aromatic and clean.

LONDON BURNING

London Burning both looks and tastes new and different. Produced at 40 per cent abv from 100 per cent grain spirit, it is redistilled with core ingredients such as juniper, coriander, angelica and cubebs. Then comes the surprise – a final distillation with lemon grass, ginger and honey. The result is a crisp English-style dry gin with lightly spiced undertones. Its producer, The Wholly Spirits Company, has also made a radical departure from the traditional in terms of the style and packaging of their brand to position it as a niche product. Look out for the wild design featuring leaping flames on the bottle in up-market cocktail bars and restaurants.

LONDON ORIGINAL DRY

The Martinelli Group, which owns the London Gin Company, was founded in 1997 by Martin Gill, an ex-tea man and serial entrepreneur. This background is evident in the development of London Original Dry, which contains bergamot, the ingredient that gives Earl Gray tea its flavour. In gin it adds a delicious smoky perfume, an unusual foil for the oily juniper and citric notes. At 40 per cent abv London Original Dry is a premium strength gin, like its sister brand, Prince's gin, more commonly known as Edinburgh gin. The group has also launched the stylishly packaged Sin & Tonic, a low-alcohol gin and tonic premix.

POLO CLUB EXTRA DRY

At 43 per cent abv, Polo Club is a new, high-strength brand that contains cardamom, cassia, nutmeg and liquorice as well as the traditional core botanicals. Like Bombay Dry and Bombay Sapphire, it is made by the infusion process where neutral alcohol in vapour form is passed through a berry chamber containing the botanicals. It both looks and tastes immensely stylish.

GIN FROM AROUND THE WORLD

HOLLAND

There are over two hundred brands of jenever still on the market, including fruit-flavoured ones. Many are very localised, produced locally and sold in the local pub, and the market is dominated by 15 major producers of whom the largest are De Kuypers, Bols and Heineken.

DE KUYPERS

De Kuypers was founded in 1695 in Schiedam, the home of the jenever industry, and is still based there. In addition to producing jenevers in

Holland such as their excellent jonge Graanjenever and an oude jenever still sold in the traditional stone crocks, it has a subsidiary in Montreal and licensed production in other countries including the USA. Under the guidance of an English distiller, De Kuypers has recently started production of a London Dry style gin but the company is known principally for its extensive range of liqueurs including Peachtree, the largest liqueur brand in the world.

BOLS

Lucas Bols set up his Amsterdam distillery in 1572, making it the longest-established distillery in the Netherlands. At its present vast premises in Zoetermeer outside The Hague, Bols makes a range of different types of jenever including Bokma, Coebergh Bessenjenever (blackcurrant flavoured), Hoppe and speciality jenevers matured in oak, such as Bokma Royal Dark, Bokma Vif Jaren and Bols Corenwyn. They also make Bols Silver Top, a dry gin that is close to the London Dry style but sweeter and more aromatic.

OTHER BRANDS

Other brands from Schiedam-based distilleries to watch out for: Distilleerderij Dirzwager owns the Floryn jenever brand and makes Leyden Dry gin; UTO Nederland BV makes Vlek jenever and Notaris; Jeneverstokerij Nolet makes the famous Ketel I; and the Museum Distillery produces an extremely good traditional maltwine jenever. From outside Schiedam, you could look for Boomsma Graanjenever, Verhoeven jenever made by UD, and the oude jenever and korenwyn produced by the Hulsink distilleries. Delft, which was once the other great centre for distilling now has only one distillery, Bestnat BV, which produces jenever and other traditional Dutch spirits.

Havenkerk. Schiedam.

Uitg. Henri Rebers, Schiedam.

129

BELGIUM

In Belgium the traditions and history of jenever
production, which first took shape in the 1600s,
are essentially the same as those of Holland. Today
there are about a score of jenever producers in
Belgium making 150 different spirits, in both
old and young styles.

FILLIERS

Small brand and family-owned distillery at
Deinze. The grain mix is wheat, rye and malt

and the production
methods are un-
changed since the
1800s. The spirit
ages in oak casks and
the company markets
both a five- and an
eight-year-old —
unique apparently,
in the entire Belgian,
Dutch and German
jenever industries.
Filliers house style is
drawn from the rye
content in its cereal
mix; the jenever is
rich, fragrant and
well mellowed.

HOOREBEKE

Belgium's oldest jenever brand and company. Van Hoorebeke was founded in 1740, at the time when jenever was starting to be made to a more-or-less fixed routine. The Van Hoorebeke family was originally from Oudenarde, in East Flanders, and since 1400, its business had been first brewing, then distilling.

Other brands of note: Meyboom of the Fourcroy firm is one of the new-generation jenevers designed to target younger, image-conscious consumers; Peket De Houyeu, a premium brand from Bouillon, is an old jenever, with colour from oak ageing; and Smeets, a staple young jenever, has been produced in the Hasselt district of Belgium since 1947.

Above left
Three generations of the Van Hoorebeke family.

THE UNITED STATES

Opposite
Fleischmann's
was the first
American
distiller to
produce a dry
gin.

In the United States the newer brands of English gin such as Bombay Sapphire, which was essentially invented for the American market, have led the revival of gin's fortunes and a resurgence of cocktail culture. Imported English gin is still the most prestigious and sales of premium brands like Tanqueray and Beefeater continue to increase every year. That is not to say there are no very good American-produced London Dry types of gin. Fleischmann's, for instance, was established in Ohio by the Fleischmann brothers in 1870 and was the first American distillers to produce a dry gin. The triple distilled Union Jack is another good brand.

Many UK companies produce their brands in the States. UDV has two distilleries in America producing Gordon's gin for the home market at 40 per cent abv or 80 proof. Gilbey's does the same. Tanqueray recently launched a new expression called Tanqueray Malacca, a spicier, more aromatic gin than usual aimed at the Afro-American market and available only in the USA. The biggest-selling brand, however, is the American-owned Seagram's.

*FIRST GIN DISTILLED IN AMERICA · DISTILLED FROM AMERICAN GRAIN · 90 PROOF · THE FLEISCHMANN DISTILLING CORPORATION, PEEKSKILL, NEW YORK.

SEAGRAM'S EXTRA DRY

Seagram's Extra Dry gin is number one in the United States, outselling the second, third and fourth largest-selling brands combined, with over 4 million 9-litre cases annually. It was introduced in 1939 as Seagram's Ancient Bottle Distilled Dry gin, not exactly a name that trips off the tongue. It is notable for being the only dry gin that is specially aged in white oak casks. Light, crisp and delicately flavoured with strong citrus notes, Seagram's Extra Dry is distilled from grain and bottled at 40 per cent abv.

BOODLES

Boodles is a traditional British brand dating back to 1847 but now bottled in the States. Produced at 90 proof it is a high-strength, very dry gin with citrus and spice notes.

SEAGRAM-DISTILLERS COMPANY. N. Y. C. 90 PROOF. DISTILLED DRY GIN. DISTILLED FROM AMERICAN GRAIN.

Let's settle the martini argument, once and for all.

It takes extra-dry gin to make an extra-dry martini.

But what if you could have _more_ than just dryness in a gin?
What if you could find a gin that's so dry
it almost crackles — but doesn't stop there?
A gin that's been nurtured through a costly extra step
that removes excess sweetness and perfumery.
We have something to tell you:
there _is_ such a gin. Its name is Seagram's.
Makes the greatest martinis ever mixed.
And there can't be any argument about _that_.

SEAGRAM'S EXTRA DRY GIN

135

SPAIN

Spain is the second-largest international gin market and has the highest per capita consumption of gin in the world. There are many brands of Spanish gin available, though Larios is predominant. Some Spanish gins are extremely localised and vary enormously in quality.

LARIOS

Larios dominates the domestic market and is indeed the fourth-biggest seller worldwide. The Larios family moved to Malaga at the beginning of the 19th century. Initially they were involved in cane processing, then subsequently built up a business empire based on textiles, transport, banking, soap manufacture, mining and a host of other commodities. In 1865 Martin Larios was made the Marques of Larios.

The company got involved in distilling by acquiring the firm of

Jimenez & Lamothe, wine makers and distillers of brandy, in 1916. Facing ruin after phylloxera, Larios joined forces with E Crooke y Cia, which was already involved in distilling compound spirits. Larios SA, as it was now known, started producing gin in 1933.

Larios gin calls itself a London Dry and is very much in that style in that is it is double distilled, aromatic and unsweetened, with strong juniper tastes. Like most Spanish gins it is bottled at 40 per cent abv. Occasionally one can detect a cane spirit aftertaste but somehow it doesn't seem to matter, particularly after a couple of Spanish-style gin and tonics when nothing much seems to matter. The company has its imitators and a general rule is to avoid the ones that too closely model themselves on the Larios branding and packaging – not that one feels too sorry for Larios as their branding is virtually identical to that used by Gordon's for their export gin.

GIN GIRO

Gin Giro is made in Barcelona and bottled at 40 per cent. Although it is based on a cane spirit and obviously made in the cold compounded manner it is perfectly drinkable. Its flavour is sweet, very juniper and talcum-powdery, possibly because of a greater use than usual of orris.

XORIGUER GIN, GIN DE MAHON

Gin de Mahon is like Plymouth Gin in that it can be so described only if it is made in Mahon on Menorca. Gin distilling on the island dates from the 18th century when Menorca was owned by the British. Thousands of British soldiers and sailors were stationed there and to meet their demand for the newly fashionable gin, local distilleries sprang up. They imported juniper berries and distilled them with a spirit made from local wine. At the beginning of the 20th century the Pons family founded the Xoriguer distillery to transform what was essentially a local custom into a fully fledged business. The distillery, now the only one to make Gin de Mahon, is still owned by the family.

Gin de Mahon is made in the traditional manner, in copper stills heated by wood-burning fires, with juniper from Mediterranean mountains and other aromatic herbs. When distillation is complete the gin is stored in large oak barrels until it is bottled at 40 per cent abv.

Only descendants of the family know the secrets of the Gin de Mahon recipe. On tasting it has a schnapps-like flavour with strong hints of almond, caraway and orris. It is sold in bottles that, although made of glass, mimic old Dutch stone crocks with handles. Locally it is mixed with lemonade to make a drink called pomada, and no celebration on the island is complete without it.

EASTERN EUROPE

Gin is not a traditional eastern European drink for obvious reasons. It was introduced to Poland during the 18th century by Dutch sailors and soon became popular along the Baltic coast. From there it spread inland but has never threatened vodka and schnapps in eastern European countries. There are, however, some interesting brands.

POLMOS KRAKOW DRY

Made by Polmos at their distillery in Krakow using all natural ingredients and distilled in the traditional way. It's distinctively dry and not very juniper in flavour, which perhaps reflects the fact that Polmos is better known for its vodka than gin.

Right

*Jenever was
introduced to
Poland during
the 18th century
by Dutch sailors
and soon became
popular along
the Baltic coast.*

MARINE DRY

Marine Dry is made by the Zwack company in
Budapest, which has an interesting history.
Zwack is a family-owned company dating back
to 1840 when Jozsef Zwack established the first
Hungarian liqueur distillery. Its principal
product was Unicum, a herbal liqueur based on
a secret family recipe. Unicum was an instant and
roaring success and Zwack was appointed
supplier to the Hapsburg court. After the First
World War Zwack had several distilleries
throughout the Austro-Hungarian empire and

introduced other spirits including gin. The family and the company left Hungary around 1948 when all industry was being nationalised. Peter Zwack, the present head of the company, was one of the first businessmen to return and in 1989 bought back expropriated family property. Zwack is now up and running again.

Marine Dry gin is in the London Dry style, double-distilled with juniper berries. At 45 per cent abv it is exceptionally strong and spirity but its slightly sweet, not unpleasant aftertaste indicates that it is not based on a grain spirit.

THE PHILIPPINES

GINEBRA SAN MIGUEL

This is the only brand from the Philippines worth mentioning and then only because, astonishingly enough, it is the biggest-selling gin brand in the world. It sells more than 26 million 9-litre cases annually, more than all other gin brands combined. If you ever taste it, you'll wonder why. Bottled at 40 per cent it is made from a distinctly dodgy spirit that tastes like arak and is flavoured with obviously chemical compounds. However, its massive sales reflect the fact that, outside the Muslim areas in the south, Filipino social life revolves around drinking gin, usually neat with ice, which explains why they get through so much.

FLAVOURED GINS

Many of the old established distillers made flavoured gins by steeping fruit in the gins before bottling. Gordon's produced orange and lemon gins until relatively recently. The fashion for flavoured gins has returned in a big way in recent years perhaps in an attempt to re-create the success flavoured vodkas have had. Gordon's produces grapefruit-flavoured and coolmint-flavoured gins, while Seagram's has launched Grapefruit Twisted gin and Lime Twisted gin, the latter one of the fastest-growing new products in the spirits market.

BANANA GIN

A curious remnant from old trading habits. The Dutch and English used jenever and gin as a component of the shameful 'triangular trade' whereby ships took goods to West Africa, exchanged them for slaves whom they transported to the Caribbean and the Americas, and there loaded up with sugar and tobacco that they brought back to home ports. West African gins, often called banana gins, are a reminder of this. These gins contain no juniper and are essentially fruit brandies. They are principally used for ritual purposes and are often poured out on to the ground as an offering. Frankly, this is probably the best thing to do with them.

CHAPTER SIX

DRINKING GIN

There are hundreds of ways to drink gin ranging from the greatest cocktail of all time, the dry Martini, to the kopstet (literally, a blow to the head), which is the Dutch habit of drinking jonge jenever with half a pint of lager, considered by some the ultimate hangover cure.

Opposite

Following the example set by Booth's, gin advertising in the 30s focused on popular recipes for gin drinks.

GIN AND TONIC

In reality, the way most people encounter gin is via the gin and tonic. Gin and tonic water is one of those combinations that seem made for each other, the clean taste of the gin enhancing the aromatic bitterness of the tonic in a drink that is subtle, refreshing and quintessentially English. And, like other irredeemably English institutions – tea, suburban bungalows, pyjamas and kedgeree – the gin and tonic owes its existence to the British presence in India.

Traditionally the principal flavouring of Indian tonic water or quinine tonic water (the terms are interchangeable) is a quinine salt rendered soluble in citric acid. Other bitter ingredients may also be used – cassia, for example, or gentian, chiretta and horehound. The name quinine comes from quina, the Peruvian word for the bark of a tree. Spanish invaders found natives using the bark of the cinchona tree as a cure for fever, particularly malaria, and began using it themselves, calling it cinchon or Jesuit's bark. By the 18th century cinchon had reached Spain and Italy, and its fame had spread even further. On the instructions of the Dutch, the German explorer Dr Hasskari took seeds of the tree from South America to Indonesia and, from about 1867 onwards, cinchona was cultivated in Java, India, Ceylon and Jamaica. Quinine was used to both prevent and treat malaria in the tropics. In India the bitter flavour of the quinine was made palatable by adding sugar and diluting the mixture with soda water and lemon juice.

And now the other half of the perfect combination comes into place. The British had always used gin as a trading commodity in India. Gin was very much part of the British way of life in the Raj – part memory of home and all things British, part consolation, and part indulgence. It wasn't long before someone had the bright idea of enlivening the daily medicinal dose of quinine with gin.

Returning ex-pats brought the taste for this exotic, bitter drink home with them. Surprisingly, because one tends to think of proprietary bottled drinks as a modern convenience, commercial production of what were called 'tonic brewed drinks' began as long ago as the mid-19th century. In 1858, Erasmus Bond patented 'an improved aerated tonic liquid' specifying the use of quinine and other flavouring agents including bitter orange. Soon there were many brands of tonic water on the market, with Schweppes adding Indian tonic water to its range in the 1870s.

Tonic water for the UK and European market still contains just enough quinine to impart the characteristic bitter flavour but higher proportions are used in the tropics in recognition of its medicinal value. Until Schweppes started bottling it in the States under franchise in 1953, tonic water remained very much a British taste. Nowadays, of course, it is truly international, appreciated everywhere both on its own and mixed with spirits such as tequila, vodka and particularly gin.

A properly made gin and tonic is one of life's great pleasures. It should be ice cold and bitter clean with a sharp bite to it. Sadly in most pubs and bars this elixir has been as rare as hens' teeth. Not for much longer one hopes. Gordon's, for example, has invested a great deal of the money they saved by reducing the abv of their brand in raising the profile of gin. A particular success has been the drive to promote the perfect gin and tonic. Thanks to this, consumers are no longer content to be fobbed off with a pub gin and tonic – an inadequate measure of a pouring brand with sweet, flat tonic and half-melted ice topped with a sliver of lemon that has been sitting on the counter all day.

THE PERFECT GIN AND TONIC

With just a few basic rules you can have a drink that approaches perfection:

- Always use a good-quality London Dry gin, kept in the freezer for extra coldness.
- Never use tonic from a spray gun or a bottle that has been standing opened. Your tonic water should always be a freshly opened bottle of Schweppes. Open a litre bottle only if you intend to use it all immediately. Do not be tempted by diet versions.
- Take a tall glass with a heavy bottom (which makes the bubbles in the tonic last longer). If there's time, frost the glass in the freezer beforehand.
- Ice is crucial. At home you should use large chunks of ice made from filtered or bottled water and pat them dry with a tea towel. Put 2 or 3 chunks in the glass and add a generous measure of gin.
- Pour in enough tonic to fill the glass. What you're aiming for is just over double the amount of tonic to gin.
- Add a freshly cut wedge of lemon, if you wish, or, for a slightly different flavour, lime. (Some gin experts claim that lemon or lime spoils the flavour, particularly of a citrus-laden gin like Beefeater which is better without any extra citrus.)
- Stir to release the juniper flavour. Bliss!

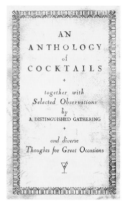

AN
ANTHOLOGY
of
COCKTAILS
+
together with
Selected Observations
by
A. DISTINGUISHED GATHERING
+
and diverse
Thoughts for Great Occasions

The point about a gin and tonic is that it is the perfect early evening drink. In fact the same is true of all gin-based drinks. They allow one to reflect on the achievements or disasters of the day with equanimity, and pass those potentially anxious hours between the end of work and dinner at peace with the world and oneself. This effect is partly physiological – of all the common liquors gin gives the quickest lift – and partly psychological – gin has been associated with the hours of ease at the end of the day for most of this century.

Our choice for
HON BRIAN LEWIS

> BOOTHS GIN
> APRICOT BRANDY
> KINA LILLET
> 2 Dashes ABSINTHE
> *Shake well and strain into cocktail glass.*

Thought for the occasion:
"CHANGE YOUR GEARS BUT NOT YOUR GIN. BOOTHS WILL CARRY YOU UP ANY HILL."

Our choice for
THE LADY MOUNT TEMPLE

> BOOTHS GIN
> ORANGE JUICE
> APRICOT BRANDY
> 1 Dash CLOVE SYRUP
> *Shake well and strain into cocktail glass.*

Thought for the occasion:
INVITATION IS THE SINCEREST FORM OF FLATTERY, ESPECIALLY AN INVITATION TO BOOTHS.

LADY MOUNT TEMPLE considers:
"I WANT GOOD MIXERS AT MY PARTIES AND SO I ALWAYS INSIST ON MIXING THEM WITH BOOTHS."

GIN COCKTAILS

Opposite

The publication of Booth's An Anthology of Cocktails, in which the cream of society gave their favourite cocktail recipes, firmly placed the 'scene' in British culture.

The classic definition of a cocktail (found in all bar tending manuals) is 'an iced drink made of spirits, bitters, flavouring and sugar'. In practice this tends to be a base, a modifier which is either bitters or another liquor, fruit, carbonated drinks and/or fruit juice. The reason why so many (over 7,000) cocktails are based on gin is that what is required of the base is that it should have its own distinctive taste yet be able to blend with other flavours. Gin does this.

Gin cocktails traditionally divide into two types – the aromatic and the sour. Aromatic cocktails use bitters such as Angostura or one of the various aromatic wines such as French or Italian vermouth, or both. Dry sherry is sometimes used instead of aromatic wine and aromatic liqueurs, Benedictine or Chartreuese for example, can be added.

PINK GINS

A typical aromatic cocktail is the pink gin, where several drops of Angostura bitters are swirled around a glass and any surplus shaken out. Then $1^1/_2$ measures of Plymouth gin and some ice are added. In British India, pink gin became a gin piaj by the addition of tiny onions marinated in chilli. Another Raj cocktail is the gin pahit, where an old fashioned glass is filled with gin to within 1cm of the top, then 3 dashes of Angostura bitters,

2 dashes of absinthe and ice are added. One tends to think of the combination of gin and absinthe as lethal but it is quite commonly found.

There are other popular aromatic cocktails:

GIN 'N' IT

Make in the same way as the gin pahit above, but use 3 parts gin to 1 part Italian vermouth instead of all gin.

THE GLOOM CHASER/
THE MONKEY GLAND

Make the same way as a dry martini (see page 158), but add 2 dashes of absinthe and 2 dashes of grenadine to the shaker before stirring.

THE BRONX

Shake together 1 part French vermouth, 1 part Italian vermouth, 1 part orange juice and 6 parts gin with cracked ice. Drop a twist of orange peel into each glass.

The definitive aromatic cocktail, indeed the definitive cocktail of all time, is the dry martini. One hesitates to say a single word here about the martini when whole books have been written on the subject: cultural theories have been dedicated to it; people have come to blows about it. It is the most discussed, debated and praised cocktail in history.

The dry martini is indisputably American, indeed the humorist H L Mencken described it as 'the only American invention as perfect as the sonnet'. As with everything else to do with the martini, its provenance is a minefield of rumour and misinformation. It is likely that it was invented in the decade following the end of the Civil War since a drink called the martinez was already popular enough to feature in bartenders' manuals of the 1880s. In 1888 Harry Johnson's manual was the first to spell it martini. By the 1890s martini had edged out martinez and was a common recipe generally specifying a mixture of gum syrup, bitters, Old Tom gin, red Italian vermouth and a squeeze of lemon peel. Tooth-rotting perhaps, and light years away from the dry martini as we know it, but that significant union of gin and vermouth had been made.

Over time the recipe became less sweet. An 1893 recipe gives the proportions as 1 dash of orange bitters and $2/3$ Plymouth gin to $1/3$ French vermouth. Plymouth is a dry, unsweetened gin and French vermouth is aromatic and also unsweetened. Confusingly, this drink was described as a Marquerite, a name that shortly disappeared from bartenders' menus. In 1910 a bartender (even more confusingly, called Signor Martini) working at New York's Knickerbocker Hotel was serving this combination as the dry martini and so it has been known ever since.

The dry martini is a real drinker's drink.

Question: Why is a dry martini like a woman's breasts?

Answer: Because one is not enough and three is too many.

Dry martinis are hard core and no other drink can make you really drunk really fast the way a martini can – making and drinking a dry martini is a test of manhood. As the famous martini historian Barnaby Conrad says: 'Martini culture is not about getting drunk and slipping under the table. It's about grace under pleasure.'

In the fifties and sixties the dry martini was the drink of corporate America and hence of the international businessman. The dry martini defined American culture both at home and abroad and was celebrated in literature, music and, above all, in Hollywood. During the Cold War Khrushchev even described it as 'America's lethal weapon'.

Throughout the seventies and eighties the dry gin martini lost pole position, mainly as the result of the emergence of vodka as the cool drink of the time but partly also because the sixties' generation saw it as the drink of their parents and rejected it as conventional and bourgeois. The baby boomers had other ways of getting high and there is a fantastic irony about the outrage this caused among a generation that often nightly consumed half a bottle of gin per person. Jimmy Carter's denunciation of free-

<u>Most popular</u> at any party...a Gordon's Martini!

There's no Gin like **GORDON'S**

loading fat cats and their three-martini lunches dealt the martini a further blow. The new puritanism, with its no-drinking, no-smoking, natural food and exercise obsession, almost sounded its death-knell. But hey! – the word on the street is that the gin martini is back, in all its glory.

There is a fashion for calling any drink served in a martini glass a martini. Fight it. Strictly speaking a dry martini is a martini only when it is made with a premium London Dry gin and French, not Italian, vermouth.

There has always been much argument as to the correct way to make the dry martini. At one end of the divide are those who advocate a standard 4:1 gin to vermouth ratio. At the other end are Martini aficionados like the film-maker Luis Buñuel who advised 'simply allowing a ray of sunlight to shine through a bottle of Noilly Prat before it hits the bottle of gin'. One hesitates to stick one's head over the parapet but what should be considered is, at what point the dry martini is still a cocktail and not just a glass of cold neat gin with a spray of lemon juice? For my money that point is reached when a dry martini is made as follows:

Opposite
60s martini chic.

Below
Gordon's, like many other gin companies, produced ready mixes for a range of cocktails including the martini.

THE DRY MARTINI

Into a cold metal shaker half-filled with ice pour 1 part good-quality French vermouth at room temperature to 7 parts premium-brand ice-cold London Dry gin. Stir vigorously and pour into chilled, V-shaped martini glasses. Twist lemon peel over the top and add an olive, preferably one previously soaked in gin.

THE GIBSON

Make as for the dry martini, but substitute a small pickled cocktail onion for the olive and lemon.

The current cocktail revival is centred around new urban-style bars and designer restaurants where the dry martini has been reinvented, often in ways that have the purists frothing at the mouth. The smoky martini, for example, adds between a dash to ¹/₂ fl oz of whisky to the basic mix; the dirty martini includes a splash of olive brine. Then there's the Molotov, a basic dry martini with a lemon or orange twist flamed over the glass. The Cajun martini mixes gin infused with jalapeño chillies with dry vermouth and a pepper garnish. Martini bores may get on their high horses but there is no reason why each generation should not redefine this classic for itself. The martini is a big enough drink to survive.

The other main ingredient of the martini is vermouth, from wermut, the German name for its principal flavouring, wormwood. Vermouth is white wine, blended, fortified and made aromatic through the addition of macerated herbs and spices, chiefly the flowers of wormwood (its leaves are used to make absinthe). There are three kinds of vermouth: Italian, such as Martini & Rossi and Cinzano, Savoie vermouth, and southern French, typically Noilly Prat, which is the best for dry martinis.

Below
*The Singapore
Sling.*

THE SOURS
Sour cocktails contain lemon or lime juice, spirits and sugar or another sweetener. They are closely related to the Collins family and the slings of Victorian England. A typical sour is the gimlet.

THE GIMLET
Shake together 3 parts gin to 1 part Rose's lime juice in a shaker with ice. Pour.

The Singapore sling is another of the world's great combinations and originates from the famous Raffles hotel in Singapore. It provides opportunities for almost endless experimentation based on the recipe below.

THE SINGAPORE SLING
Shake together 1 teaspoon sugar syrup, 2 fl oz fresh lime juice, 2 fl oz London Dry gin and a dash of

Angostura bitters. Strain into an 8 fl oz highball glass with crushed ice. Add $^1/_2$ fl oz Cointreau and $^1/_2$ fl oz cherry brandy. Top up the glass with soda water. A slice of lemon peel should be twisted over the drink and then dropped into the glass. Stir well.

Then there's the white lady, supposedly dreamed up by Ernest Hemingway and F Scott Fitzgerald while on a binge in Paris.

THE WHITE LADY

Pour 1 part Cointreau or triple sec to 2 parts lemon juice into a shaker with cracked ice and 1 egg white to each two drinks. Shake vigorously until thoroughly mixed. Add 4 parts gin, combine and shake. Then add a further 4 parts gin and shake well. Strain into chilled cocktail glasses and serve. For a Pink Lady substitute 4 teaspoons of grenadine for the Cointreau and omit the lemon juice.

THE NEGRONI

Basically a sling, this drink consists of equal parts of gin, sweet vermouth and Campari. Pour the ingredients into a tall glass over ice and add soda water if desired. Stir and add half a slice of orange.

MIXED DRINKS

In addition to the two basic types of cocktail, the aromatic and the sour, there are also distinct variations between true cocktails and mixed drinks. Gin and tonic, for example, is a mixed drink. The Tom Collins is another and, for those who find the taste of tonic water overpowering, it's a delicious and refreshing alternative made as follows:

THE TOM COLLINS

Squeeze the juice of a lemon into a tall Collins glass. Add 1 heaped teaspoon sugar, 2 fl oz gin and plenty of ice. Top up the glass with soda water.

The confusion that exists between the Tom Collins and the John Collins is not helped by the fact that the original John Collins was made with Old Tom style gin. In fact, when made with dry gin, there is no difference between the two drinks. However, a John Collins is now more commonly made with whisky. The gin Rickey is first cousin to a Collins, but made with fresh lime juice rather than lemon juice and no sugar. It was the invention of a barman at the Shoemakers Restaurant in Washington at the turn of the century. The first person to try it was a Colonel Jim Rickey – hence the name.

1769: Gordon's Gin

The fad was more "Fop" than "Mod" when Londoner Alexander Gordon developed his fabulous gin recipe. But the thing for gin to be then was the same thing gin should be now. Dry! Gordon's is so dry it's known as the "martini gin" to many a pernickety martini-ite. Biggest seller in England, America, the world.

1968: Gordon's 'Cranaby St.'

Psychedelic in color. Light, sassy, delicious in taste. A tall, lanky drink that's tart and tingling. Start with a tall, slim glass. Add ice and the juice of ½ a lemon. Pour in 1½ oz. of Glorious Gordon's Gin and 3 oz. of cranberry juice. Add two drops of bitters and a splash of soda water. Stir.

What will the English think of next?

THE ORANGE BLOSSOM

This is a mixed drink that combines gin with orange juice and orange flower water. It is essentially a Screwdriver made with gin.

1 ¾ oz gin, 1 ¾ oz fresh orange juice and a dash of orange flower water. Shake and strain into a cocktail glass.

In the 50s popular mixers for gin lower down the social scale were traditionally peppermint cordial, orange squash and ginger beer. Nowadays the favourites for gin are bitter lemon, orange juice and, of course, tonic water. Each has its own image, with gin and tonic still considered the choice of the golf-playing, Jag-driving set, and gin and orange the ultimate 'tarts' drink. In Spain, where they do things differently, the most popular mixer for gin is Coca-Cola.

One should not forget the role Dutch jenever still has to play as the second cousin of gin, particularly in an international context. Although it is not as good a mixer as London Dry gin, it is possible to create some interesting combinations with the more neutral styles of jonge jenever.

THE AMSTERDAM

Pour 1 measure of jonge jenever in a cocktail shaker with a ½ measure of triple sec, a ½ measure of grapefruit juice and ice. Shake and serve in cocktail glasses.

Sloe gin and Pimm's are both traditional English gin drinks. Sloe gin is a British liqueur made using wild sloe berries, the fruit of the blackthorn tree, through a steeping process that goes back to the 17th century. Two companies produce sloe gin commercially – Gordon's and Plymouth, which makes Hawker's Sloe Gin. Both could sell their production three times over as sloe gin is extremely popular, particularly with the hunting, fishing and shooting set. Because sloes grow only in the wild, it is virtually impossible to increase production and demand always outstrips supply. However, sloe gin is easily made at home.

SLOE GIN

Gather your sloe berries. Half-fill a gin bottle with sloes, add 5 cm/2 inches of caster sugar and top up with full-strength gin. Leave for about 3 months, shaking the bottle every now and then, and there you have it.

Pimm's was invented in London in the 19th century at the Pimm's restaurant and was based on a recipe of gin blended with liqueurs, herbs and spices. In 1859 James Pimm started bottling his famous drink and selling it to bars and restaurants. Other Pimm's cups based on Scotch, rum, rye whisky and brandy were introduced, but the gin-based Pimm's No 1 remains the quintessential English summer drink.

GIN IN THE KITCHEN

Gin drinks are generally seen as a prelude to food because they do what an aperitif or sundowner does best, which is to sharpen the appetite and refresh the palate. However, since Asian and Pacific Rim styles of cuisine have become popular, gin is becoming a fashionable accompaniment to food. A long, cold glass of gin and tonic goes perfectly with Thai food, for example, and is a far better taste partner than wine for most styles of Asian food because the spicy, dry flavours of each complement the other.

Because of its strong, predominantly juniper flavour, gin's culinary applications are more restricted than other spirits, but it does have its uses. Flavouring meat with eau de vie de genièvre is a common feature of northern French and Belgian regional cooking and gin is good with all types of game. It will also enhance the flavour of any dish with juniper berries as an ingredient, such as pork pâté, where the addition of 2 dessertspoons of gin make this rather ordinary dish more glamorous. Gin and tomatoes are a good combination – which is perhaps not altogether surprising because, until vodka replaced it, gin and tomato juice made up the classic bloody Mary.

When using gin in the kitchen it is important not to skimp on quality by using an own-label or inferior brand. Cooking and reducing with gin removes its alcoholic content not its flavour, which brings out the worst in a poor-quality gin, so unfortunately there's no such thing as 'cooking gin'.

Opposite
*Jenever, food
and conversation
in a Dutch inn,
17th century.*

RECIPES

GIN SALAD DRESSING
The Dressing
Mix 100 ml good quality gin, 1 teaspoon salt, 1 teaspoon castor sugar, freshly ground black pepper
2 tablespoons olive oil

The Salad
Slice tomatoes, black olives, onion, finely shred lettuce.

Pour dressing over salad and serve.

JUNIPER GIN GAME SAUCE

Juniper flavours combine extremely well with game such as pheasant and grouse. Because game tends to dry out when cooked, a sauce like this is perfect with roasted game dishes.

250 ml/8 fl oz chicken stock
120 ml/4 fl oz red wine
120 ml/4 fl oz dry gin
45 ml/3 tbsp balsamic vinegar
30 ml/2 tbsp juniper berries, crushed
7.5 ml/1 tsp coarsely ground black pepper
1 bay leaf
arrowroot, to thicken

Combine all the ingredients except the arrowroot in a medium-sized saucepan. Bring to a boil and simmer until the liquid is reduced to the texture of a good gravy. Remove the bay leaf, turn up the heat and add a little arrowroot to thicken. Serve with roasted game.

CHICKEN WITH GIN AND JUNIPER

25 g/1 oz butter
4 chicken breast fillets
1 medium onion, peeled and diced
1 garlic clove, crushed
15 ml/1 tbsp chopped parsley
15 ml/1 tbsp honey

15 ml/1 tbsp mustard
250 ml/8 fl oz chicken stock
120 ml/4 fl oz red wine
60 ml/4 tbsp gin
15 ml/1 tbsp juniper berries, lightly crushed

Melt the butter and sauté the chicken until browned. Transfer to an ovenproof dish. Cook the onion until soft. Blend together the remaining ingredients and add to pan. Heat through and pour over the chicken. Cover and cook in the oven for about 40 minutes at a medium to high heat. Serve with rice.

CABBAGE WITH GIN AND JUNIPER

1–1 1/2 cabbage cut lengthwise into 6 wedges leaving the core intact.
2 shallots chopped
6 juniper berries
1 tsp dried summer savory mix
1/4 cup butter
1/3 cup gin

Steam the cabbage in a covered steamer for 7–10 minutes or until tender but still al dente. In a large skillet melt the butter and cook the shallots with the juniper berries and savory for 10 minutes over a low heat. Stir occasionally. Add the gin, salt and pepper to taste and simmer for a further 1 minute. Add the cabbage with a slotted spoon to a heated serving dish and pour the pan juices over it before serving.

PRUE IRVINE'S GIN AND ORANGE JELLY

For adults only!

1 large can of mandarin orange segments in natural juice
100 ml/3 fl oz gin
Fresh orange juice
45 ml/3 tbsp caster sugar
1 sachet of gelatine
30 ml/2 tbsp warm water

Drain the mandarin oranges, reserving the juice, and put in a bowl or mould. Add the gin to the mandarins. Pour the reserved juice into a measuring jug and make up to 600 ml/1 pint with fresh orange juice. Add the sugar to the juice and warm very slowly in a pan until it dissolves. Dissolve the gelatine in the water and add to the mandarins with the sweetened juice. Stir gently and leave to cool, then cover with clingfilm and transfer to the fridge. Chill until set, then serve with ice cream or crème fraîche.

GIN PLACES

GREAT PLACES TO DRINK MARTINIS

5757, The Four Seasons Hotel, 57 E57th Street, New York
Bemelmans Bar, The Carlyle, 35 E56th Street, New York
The Met Bar, Metropolitan, Old Park Lane, London W1
Claridges Bar, Claridges, Brook Street, London W1
American Bar, Savoy, London W1
The Reform Bar & Grill, Spring Gardens, King Street,
    Manchester

GREAT PLACES TO DRINK GIN AND TONIC

The Lanesborough, 1 Lanesborough Place, London SW1
Harry's Bar, Calle Vallaresso, San Marco, Venice
The Galle Face Hotel, Galle Face Road, Colombo, Sri Lanka
Bar Ten, 10 Mitchell Lane, Glasgow
The Mount Nelson Hotel, 76 Orange Street, Cape Town,
    South Africa

GREAT PLACES TO DRINK GIN

Raffles Hotel, Orchard Spring Lane, Singapore
The Crown Bar, 46 Great Victoria Street, Belfast
The Outhouse Bar, 12a Broughton Street Lane, Edinburgh
The Point Hotel, 35-50 Bread Street, Edinburgh
The Palace Bar, 21 Fleet Street, Dublin
Jamzen on the Cliffs, Cousins Cove by Negril, Jamaica
Cafe Vian, Liszt ferenc ter 9, Budapest, Hungary
The Buddha Bar, 8 rue de Boissy d'Anglas, Paris

GREAT PLACES TO DRINK JENEVER

Hooghoudt, Reguliersgracht 11, Amsterdam
Cafe de Jaren, Nieuwe Doelenstraat, Amsterdam
Restaurant de Noordmolen, Noordvest 38, 3111 PH
    Schiedam

DISTILLERY VISITS

The National Distillery Museum in Schiedam has an impressive archive and working distillery where they make their own brand of jenever in the traditional way.
National Distillery Museum, Lange Gaven 74–76, Schiedam
Tel: 0031 10 426 1291

The Blackfriars Distillery, Britain's oldest working distillery where Plymouth Gin is produced, has a permanent exhibition and runs guided tours.
The Blackfriars Distillery, 60 Southside Street, Plymouth
Tel: 01752 667 062

BIBLIOGRAPHY

BAYLEY, Stephen, *Gin*, The Gin and Vodka Association of GB
BROOME, Dave, *Spirits & Cocktails*, Carlton Books Ltd
DOXAT, John, *The Gin Book,* Quiller Press
HARRISON, Brian, *Drink and the Victorians*, Faber & Faber
KINROSS, Lord, *The Kindred Spirit*, Newman Neame Ltd
RAY, Cyril, *The Complete Book of Spirits and Liqueurs*, Cassell

INDEX

PICTURE ACKNOWLEDGEMENTS

The Advertising Archives 6, 92, 99, 133, 135, 160, 163
Bombay Sapphire 72, 115,116
Greenalls 65, 69, 106
Mary Evans 16–17, 23, 30–31, 35, 43, 44, 46–47, 166
United Distillers and Vintners Archive, Leven 37, 48, 50, 51, 53, 57, 59, 60, 67, 68, 75, 78, 79, 82, 83, 95, 96, 100, 101, 102, 103, 104, 105, 110, 111, 112, 113, 144, 150, 156, 157, 165
Vin Mag Archive 55
Eric Weller 42